BRISTOL

T.H.B. Burrough

Studio Vista

Produced by November Books Limited, 23–9 Emerald Street, London, WC1N 3QL

Published by Studio Vista Limited, Blue Star House, Highgate Hill, London, N19

Text set by Yendall & Company Limited, Riscatype House, 22–5 Red Lion Court, Fleet Street, London, EC4

Printed by Compton Printing Limited, Pembroke Road, Stocklake, Aylesbury, Bucks.

SBN 289.79804.3

This book is dedicated to the Bristol Civic Society (formerly the Kyrle Society), the Council for the Preservation of Ancient Bristol, and all other societies and groups of interested persons who do so much to make Bristolians aware of the treasures that surround them, and to ensure, by their influence, that these treasures may be held in trust for future generations.

Books on Bristol

John Latimer, *The Annals of Bristol*, a) *Eighteenth Century*, b) *Nineteenth Century*. Bristol, 1891 and 1887.

C. F. W. Dening, *The Eighteenth Century Architecture of Bristol*. Bristol and London, J. W. Arrowsmith, 1923.

J. Storrs Fry and Sons, *English City: The Growth and Future of Bristol* (the text by Harold G. Brown, based on researches by Elizabeth Ralph). Bristol, Somerdale, 1945.

Tudor Edwards, *Bristol*. London and New York, B. J. Batsford, 1951.

Walter Ison, *The Georgian Buildings of Bristol*. London, Faber and Faber, 1952.

Nikolaus Pevsner, *The Buildings of England – North Somerset and Bristol*. Harmondsworth, Penguin, 1958.

Bryan Little, *The City and County of Bristol*. Bristol, Local Historical Society, 1954.

Reece Winstone, *Bristol As It Was* (series). Bristol, R. Winstone, 1961–8.

INTRODUCTION

Bristol is different from other cities. A county in its own right since 1373, it was the second city in England until overtaken by the industrial giants of the north in the late 18th century, and was England's major port, from which the Cabots set sail in 1497, and where Brunel built the first Atlantic liners. Liverpool and Manchester have taken Bristol's supremacy and at the time of writing there is a threat that the harbour will be closed to commercial traffic and increasingly covered over. However, with the port of Avonmouth only six miles down river, Bristol will remain a hub of international trade.

Apart from shipping, Bristol's strength has lain in the variety of its industries, for with the support of Fry's chocolates, Wills' cigarettes, dozens of manufacturing concerns with world-wide reputations, besides the wine and sugar trade, Bristol has been less affected by wars and slumps than other cities, and has sustained its importance for over 1,000 years.

Like Rome, they say, Bristol is built on seven hills. At any rate, the old High Cross stood on a mound surrounded by hills so that, even now, one can see green fields and trees from anywhere in the city centre. Conversely, one can see the city centre from all approaches to the city, and throughout history, until 10 years ago, this central mound was dominated by the towers and spires of the city churches; alas! no more. With the erection of the first tall office block in the central area, the churches lost their dominance. Now, with more tall blocks, one has to look for a glimpse of the churches between walls of concrete and glass. Not that these buildings are bad architecturally, but they should have never been there at all. In the valley that surrounds the old city under the encircling hills clusters of such buildings would have been admirable, and such a siting would have perhaps alleviated the traffic problem. But now the old city centre inside what little is left of the ancient walls can best be seen at close quarters and on foot. It is still a rewarding experience.

Even more than the hills, the river gives Bristol its character. The Avon, rising and falling with almost the highest tide in the world, between the cliffs and wooded slopes of the Gorge, skirted the old city and joined the Frome to form the castle moat. Later, the courses were slightly diverted and a 'New Cut' dug, by Napoleonic prisoners, to provide a constant level in the central Floating Harbour. Thus, throughout history, there have been ocean-going ships right in the middle of the city, and although parts of the harbour in the centre of the city have been gradually covered over, and larger ships have of necessity used Bristol's newer port of Avonmouth, unless the threat to close the city docks to commercial use is implemented Bristolians will still, as now, hear the sound of cranes and hooters at their office desks.

Clifton is another story. Enlarged as a dormitory for the spa down at the foot of the Avon Gorge, at a time when most merchants lived closer to their work, it later became a residential suburb for these same merchants, before they in turn left for the surrounding villages, and their houses deteriorated in multi-occupation. Now, gradually, the houses are being brought back to something like their former state, though still divided into many units. Thus Clifton, which the late Professor Sir Albert Richardson described as the most beautiful suburb in the world, may once more be worthy of such praise. Certainly the terraces seen from the harbour with the Suspension Bridge in the background justify it.

Bristol is perhaps different from other comparable cities in that it has retained its importance throughout its history. Thus it was a power in the Middle Ages comparable with, say, York; Clifton was a Georgian spa, and in Victorian times there were great developments in the Port. Buildings of all periods are to be seen. There are remains of early monasteries and of Elizabethan houses, Georgian squares and terraces, and unrivalled warehouses beside the docks. The city churches are as fine as those in any medieval city, and have the added interest of including examples from Norman times almost continuously up to the accession of Queen Victoria. The churches built in Clifton and in the newly developed suburbs in the 19th century have an individuality and a quality which make them worthy of comparison with those in any of our great Victorian cities.

Here it is necessary to give a word of explanation. Throughout this book, the designation 'Bristol' must not be taken literally. The Filton aircraft factories and the boot and shoe factories of Kingswood, and some of the factories of the tobacco and paper groups are in Gloucestershire, while the chocolate factories are mostly in Somerset! However, this is a technical matter, and the real boundaries of the city, if not the administrative ones, are fairly easy to see. But this book also goes further afield, and from the surrounding villages, full of fascinating buildings, the author has selected examples from Frenchay, which is outside Bristol by only the thickness of a rubble wall. For generations Bristolians have been brought out as children to play on the Common at Frenchay and to watch the cricket there, a pleasure that can no longer be enjoyed since the village club moved recently to another ground after over 100 years on the Common.

Recorded in 1257 as Fromscawe and later as Fromeshaw, meaning the wood on the Frome, Frenchay's picturesque cottages facing south over the river, built for the workers quarrying the richly coloured Pennant stone, date from Stuart times, and the fine gentlemen's mansions on the higher ground from the days of religious persecution in the 18th century. The first owners were Quakers or Unitarians and the two chapels still stand at either end of the Common, the Anglican Church being a Victorian intrusion. The vast Frenchay hospital, built at the outbreak of war as an emergency, hutted hospital, is now the centre in the south-west for plastic, thoracic and neuro-surgery, but being sited in the grounds of Frenchay Park does not encroach, even visually, on the Common.

A few buildings from other villages are discussed, chosen for their particular interest such as the only local Victorian mansion in the North-country tradition (Tyntesfield) and Butterfield's first Anglican Church (at Coalpit Heath). Otherwise all the buildings are in what appears to the stranger to be the city or suburbs of Bristol, all in the area served by the city, as opposed to the country, bus service. But Bristol is a small city and most of the buildings can be visited on foot.

Taken as a whole, the buildings of Bristol have a certain individuality. Although often part of the contemporary trend, Bristol was ahead of fashion in the early 14th century, and again in the early 20th century, with such buildings as the façade of Messrs Everards, the Central Library and the extension to the Royal Infirmary. Some of Bristol's mid-19th-century warehouses were quite unique. Otherwise, the buildings show individual variations on the fashionable themes, with a sprinkling of works by the national figures of the periods, Vanbrugh, Halfpenny, Wood, Isaac Ware, Smirke and Cockerell, and later Street, Butterfield, Pearson, Blomfield and Bodley, with Alfred Waterhouse winding up the 19th century to make way for Giles Gilbert Scott and Vincent Harris. Bristol even had an early Marcel Brueur, but this was an exhibition house and subsequently pulled down.

As would be expected, the works of the national architects differ little from those they designed elsewhere, though the warm stone from the Bath and Mendip quarries gives them a softness in keeping with the west-country air, but local architects, while influenced by fashion, produced buildings which were essentially Bristolian. This was most noticeable in Victorian times. Godwin was a Bristolian, but he moved to London, and it is as 'the greatest æsthete of them all' that he is best known. Mid-19th-century Bristol was dominated by the Foster family. The younger Foster, James, particularly in partnership with Wood, carried out an immense amount of work, mostly in Clifton, all interesting, and much of it making use of the red and brown local rubble stone which, with the warm coloured freestone dressings, gives the buildings of Bristol much of their character. However, in the 18th century there was the Paty family, whose Christ Church City is not only individual but of international quality, and who were responsible either as architects or as sculptors working for others, for many buildings in the neighbourhood. James Bridges was building in 18th-century Gothic, Underwood in Grecian, Pope in either and Dyer in any style that took his fancy, but always producing a building of interest.

Apart from the Art Nouveau examples of Everards – an outstanding building – and what is left of the Cabot Café (38 College Green), there is much good Art-and-Crafts architecture by the Bristolian Dare Bryan. His Western College is included in the text, but he also built some charming houses with wide eaves, tapering chimneys, and white-painted projecting windows, and sometimes with fibrous plaster in the gables, in what was then becoming the fashionable suburb of Leigh Woods, immediately on the far side of the Suspension Bridge. Other buildings, and at least two pubs, show his influence, rather than the influence of the more famous architect working in the same vein, C. F. A. Voysey.

But in the first half of the 20th century there is one name that outshines all others: George Oatley. C. F. W. Dening designed buildings with interesting detailing; P. Hartland Thomas designed churches in his own inimitable and evocative version of Gothic; but Sir George Oatley, by the sheer quality of his work, quite apart from its volume, was head and shoulders above them all. Henry Crisp, Godwin's partner, took on the young Oatley before the turn of the century, and before the First World War Oatley engaged Lawrence. The partnership of Oatley and Lawrence survived until dissolved in the late '30s, when the author entered into a partnership with Lawrence, and Oatley continued until his recent death in the still-surviving firm of Oatley and Brentnall. Oatley's chief patrons were the Wills family, for whom he built the University buildings, St Monica's Home of Rest, Combe Lodge, Blagdon (a vast Cotswold-Tudor mansion), the Homœopathic Hospital (also Cotswold-Tudor), two halls of residence – Manor Hall and Wills Hall, and several smaller houses. In his early years he built, after competitions, Winwick and Cardiff Mental Hospitals (in collaboration with C.

Skinner), and most hospitals in Bristol were at some time enlarged by him. In addition he was Surveyor to the Fabric of the Cathedral and to St Mary, Redcliffe, and designed All Hallows, Easton, and St Edyth's, Sea Mills. His work had majesty of scale and displayed scholarship in detailing – all of which, including screens, panelling and mouldings was designed by himself with a fat pencil on odd scraps of paper. Classical, Gothic, or a mixture of both, all bore the Oatley stamp, and no architectural tour of the city can fail to be an Oatley pilgrimage.

There seems to be little individuality in the new building. Perhaps there is, but we are too near to see it. However, examples of the many buildings erected since the war have been chosen to give as general a picture as possible, and perhaps the reader will see in these, and in other buildings which have had to be omitted for want of space, an indication that still, in its architecture, Bristol is different from other cities.

ACKNOWLEDGMENTS

The author wishes to thank all those who helped him in the preparation of this book, the owners and occupiers of many of the buildings included, and others whose general knowledge on particular matters was so superior to his own. But he wishes particularly to thank Miss Elizabeth Ralph, the City Archivist and Honorary Secretary of the Bristol and Gloucestershire Archæological Society and Chairman of the Council for the Preservation of Ancient Bristol, who read and commented on the text and provided from her archives much factual information which the author could not otherwise have obtained. He must also acknowledge the researches carried out by David Lloyd on Victorian architects and their work, and the full catalogue (now lodged with the author) of post-reformation churches in Bristol prepared by the late G. D. Gordon Hake, for over 30 years the principal of the R. W. A. School of Architecture, and Mrs Hake. He also wishes to thank Mr Wolf and his colleagues at the City Engineer's department who provided information from their records.

Illustrations for this book have been obtained through the kindness of many people, and the author wishes to thank them all. Many more offered illustrations for which there was not room, and these are also thanked. The author is particularly grateful for access to the collection of the late Ruding Bryan, an eminent local archæologist, through the kindness of his sister, who survives him.

Unfortunately, the photographers are in most cases not known, but where their names have been ascertained, they are put in parentheses after the acknowledgments.

Photographs were lent by the following:

The Dean and Chapter of Bristol Cathedral 2
Bristol Regional Buildings Record (Miss Joanna Tolmie, MA) 4, 14, 16, 67, 75, 79, 80, 106, 146
Bristol Public Relations Officer (Mr Lavery Crook, FIPRA, AMIAMA) 5, 6, 11, 12, 20, 30, 34, 45, 47, 55, 73, 78, 99
St Mary, Redcliffe, Vestry (Veale) 7
J. D. D. Burrough (photographer) 19
Headmistress of Redland High School 27
M. Burton (Harry Lacey) 36
The Architectural Review (Dell & Wainwright) 38
The City Archivist 39, 46, 50, 71, 72, 137 (R. A. Young, Ruding Bryan and others)
City Art Gallery 47
The Governors of Queen Elizabeth's Hospital 87
Lord Wraxhall 103
Port of Bristol Authority 121
Sir Percy Thomas & Son 128, 139, 140, 160 (Dan Barton)
Eric Ross, FRIBA 136
Messrs Dolcis (Edgar Hyman) 138
Messrs E. S. & A. Robinson 141, 154
Messrs Holland Hannen & Cubitt 142
Desmond Tripp 143
Louis Ward 144
Whicheloe & MacFarlane 145, 152, 159, 169 (Derek Balmer)
City Architect 137, 139, 147 (Warne), 163 (Derek Balmer), 164, 170 (R. Whiting)
Burrough & Hannam 149
Alec French & Partners 151, 158, 166 (C. & E. Photographers)
R. Towning Hill 153 (Derek Balmer), 165
Russell Diplock Associates (Warne) 155
Moxley Jenner & Partners 157
Nealon Tanner & Partners 149, 167
The remainder were taken by the author.

Drawings were lent by the following:

Sir Arthur Elton (Brunel's own lithograph) 73
City Art Gallery 2, 10, 105
Messrs C. J. Hole 115
Department of Education and Science 150
J. Maggs 156
Architects' Co-Partnership 171
Sir Percy Thomas & Son 172

The maps are based on the Ordnance Survey Map; they are reproduced with the sanction of the Controller of Her Majesty's Stationery Office and with permission from Geographia Ltd.

Sea Mills
Henleaze
Golden Hill
Stoke Bishop
Westbury Park
Durdham Down
Old Sneed Park
Sneed Park
Redland
Oak Wood
Clifton Down
Cotham
Leigh Woods
Zoological Gardens
Clifton College
Avon Gorge
Portway
Leighwoods
Hotwell Road
Cumberland Basin
River Avon
Coronation Road
Southville
Bedminster
Ashton Gate
Ashton Park
Ashton Court
Bower Ashton
Long Ashton
Bedminster Down
Parson Street
130
129
160
122
153
144
29
27
118
81
125
162
100
159
84
65
64
66
57
82
71
172
163
158
78
97
99
68
152
72
87
73
50
25
22
33
49
54
53
26
171
24
46
62
48
92
121
11
170
141

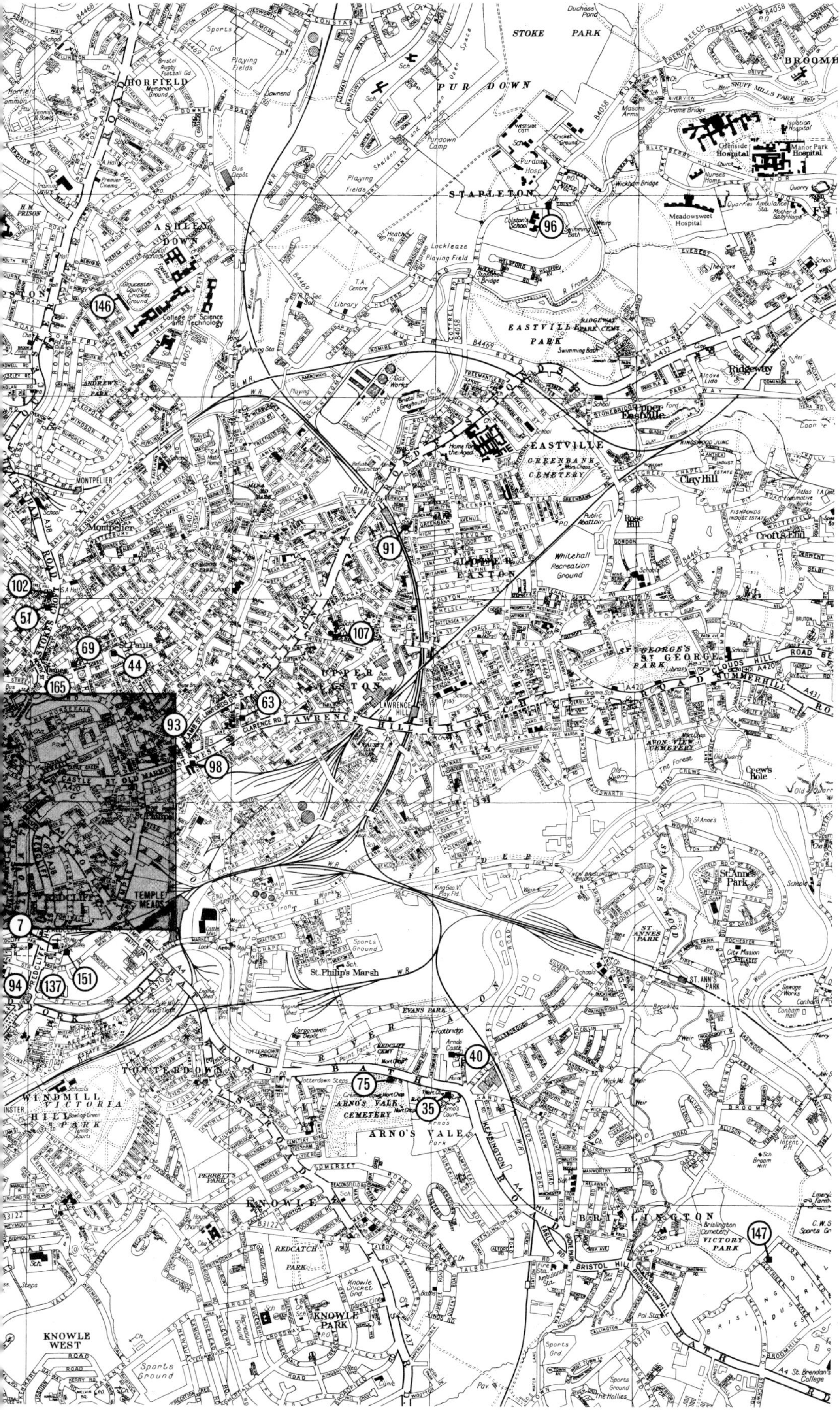
STOKE PARK
PUR DOWN
BROOMHILL
HORFIELD
STAPLETON
ASHLEY DOWN
Gloucester County Cricket Ground
College of Science and Technology
EASTVILLE PARK
Ridgeway
Upper Eastville
EASTVILLE
GREENBANK CEMETERY
Clay Hill
Rose Hill
Croft's End
Whitehall Recreation Ground
LOWER EASTON
UPPER EASTON
LAWRENCE HILL
ST GEORGE'S PARK
ST GEORGE
SUMMERHILL ROAD
MONTPELIER
Montpelier
ST ANDREW'S PARK
St Pauls
OLD MARKET
St Philips
REDCLIFF
TEMPLE MEADS
St. Philip's Marsh
FEEDER
AVON VIEW CEMETERY
Crew's Hole
St Anne's Park
ST ANNE'S WOOD
ST ANNE'S PARK
TOTTERDOWN
WINDMILL HILL
VICTORIA PARK
ARNO'S VALE CEMETERY
ARNO'S VALE
BATH ROAD
KNOWLE
PERRETT'S PARK
REDCATCH PARK
KNOWLE PARK
KNOWLE WEST
BRISLINGTON
VICTORY PARK
BRISLINGTON INDUSTRIAL ESTATE
Meadowsweet Hospital
Glenside Hospital
Manor Park Hospital
H.M. PRISON
Sports Ground
146
96
91
102
57
69
44
165
107
63
93
98
7
94
137
151
40
75
35
147

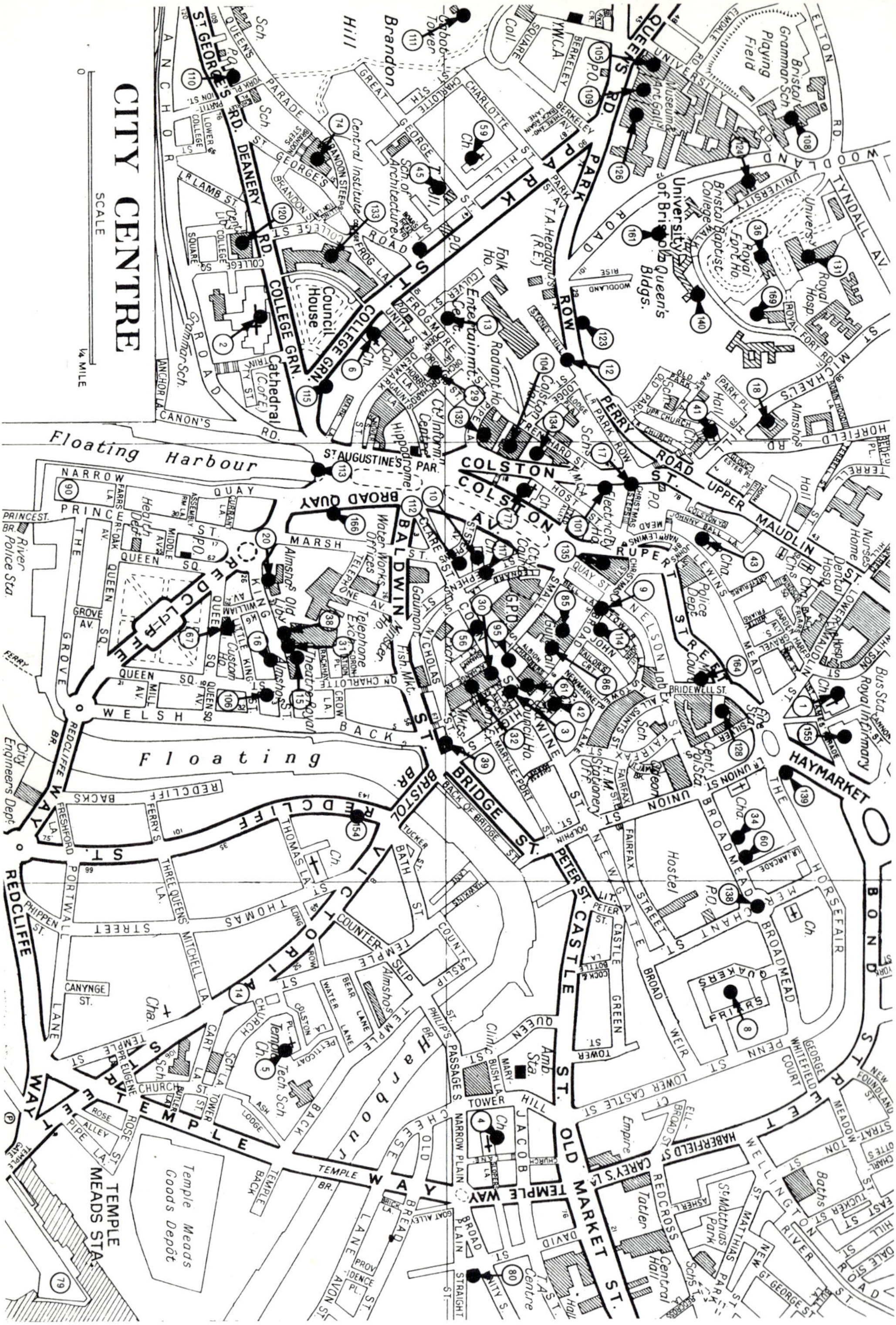

CITY CENTRE
SCALE
0
¼ MILE
Floating Harbour
Floating
Harbour
COLLEGE GRN.
Council House
Cathedral
BROAD QUAY
BALDWIN ST.
COLSTON ST.
COLSTON AV.
PARK ROW
PERRY ROAD
PARK ST.
QUEEN'S RD.
UPPER MAUDLIN ST.
HAYMARKET
BROADMEAD
RUPERT STREET
BRIDGE ST.
BRISTOL BR.
VICTORIA ST.
REDCLIFF ST.
REDCLIFFE WAY
REDCLIFFE
TEMPLE WAY
OLD MARKET ST.
CASTLE ST.
PETER ST.
UNION ST.
BOND STREET
WELSH BACK
KING ST.
MARSH ST.
QUEEN SQ.
PRINCE ST.
NARROW QUAY
ST. AUGUSTINE'S PAR.
TEMPLE MEADS STA.
Temple Meads Goods Depôt
University of Bristol
Bristol Grammar Sch.
Royal Infirmary
TYNDALL AV.
WOODLAND RD.
ST. MICHAEL'S HILL
HORSEFAIR
WELLINGTON ROAD
ST. GEORGE'S RD.
DEANERY RD.
ANCHOR RD.
CANON'S RD.

GAZETTEER

1
ST JAMES **1129 and later**
Horsefair
St James claims to be Bristol's oldest surviving church. It is all that remains of Bristol's earliest monastery, a cell of Tewkesbury, which was founded in 1129. The church nave became a parish church in 1374. Little of the original Norman work survives, and most of that has been over-restored. This cannot be said, however, of the west front which leans outward and is retained by rods behind, and is somewhat eroded. However, one can appreciate the interlaced Norman arches and especially the unusual wheel window above. This consists of a rope moulding surrounding and interlacing eight circles, themselves surrounding an inner circle with a zig-zag ring on the outside. Internally the arcades to the nave are original though much restored and not so exciting as the Norman arcades in All Saints, City, but these are visually swamped by the extentions to north and south. The south aisle dates from 1698 and is inconspicuous, but the north aisle of 1864 dominates the church. It has two rows of octagonal red granite polished pillars and elaborate capitals. There is a pleasant simple tower at the west of the south aisle. As with other Bristol churches, there is some fine plate, and also some rich and attractive monuments including the bust of T. T. Biddulph by Baily of 1842.

2
THE CATHEDRAL OF ST AUGUSTINE **1140 and later**
Bristol Cathedral, unpretentious to the passer-by, is a treasure house to the scholar. Successive centuries have contributed something that is either unique or in advance of its times, and the more important of these contributions are tabulated below.
1. The chapter house of 1142–70 is the finest Norman chapter house still standing today. It is a simple rectangle without pillars or other obstruction roofed with twin groined vaults and enriched with low-relief wall patterning and blind arcading of the period. Except for the later east wall it is today as built. There is some of the Norman work still surviving in the ante-

◀ 1

▶
2a

▶
2b
▶▶
2c

chamber, but this is much restored. Of the Augustinian abbey little more remains but the great gatehouse (late Norman 3-storeyed), an archway to the Abbot's Lodgings, and some odd remains, including a double-vaulted chamber on two pillars, in what is now the Cathedral School.

2. The chancel is one of the wonders of Gothic architecture, and was designed under the instructions of Abbot Knowle in 1298. If one

excludes the churches of Poitou, which are somewhat different in scale, this is the first hall-church of major proportions. The engineering problem of supporting the heavy vault was solved by the provision of bridges across the aisles which themselves supported small vaults set transversely. The design of these bridges is reminiscent of the crossing bracing at Wells, but this was five years later than the completion of the chancel at Bristol, so that one cannot help thinking that the Bristol masons, having completed the chancel, crossed the hills to Wells, only 20 miles away, and there worked on the strengthening of the tower arches. The chancel vault is itself unusual. Though not quite the first lierne vault, it is the first to omit the ridge-rib, thus giving a sense of net-like openness. It is also the first to enrich the ribs with cusping, and, just as the vault is enriched, so the arcading is simplified by the omission of shafting and capitals (except for two to support the vaulting), and the substitution of mouldings running uninterrupted right around the arches.

3. The ante-chapel to the Berkeley Chapel. Here, again, the vaulting is unique. In this small room the vaulting ribs are in full splendour, but support a flat ceiling, and the spaces between them are left open. The chapel is known to have been completed before 1309. The mouldings of the inner doorway are also unusual.

4. The tomb recesses in the walls are remarkable, particularly in the use of straight lines in the geometrical pattern.

5. The nave. The cathedral was left naveless since the old Norman nave was demolished, but in anticipation of the reinstatement of the diocese in 1897 a new nave was started to the designs of G. E. Street in 1868. In this design Street showed his true scholarship. He carried on the form of the 'Hall' chancel, but not the earlier mason's idiosyncrasies, and substituted orthodox early 14th-century detail. The pillars have shafts and foliated capitals: the nave vault is not lierne: the aisle 'vaultlets' are simplified and so on. The western towers were completed after his death by J. L. Pearson, who also designed the reredos.

Among the many objects of interest in the cathedral are the unique 15th-century candelabrum in the Berkeley Chapel (preserved from the bombed Temple Church), and the heavy silver candlesticks by G. Sleath, 1712, presented by John Rumsey after the successful privateering voyage of his notorious Captain, Woodes Rogers (who lived in Queen Square) on which he rescued 'Robinson Crusoe'.

3

ALL SAINTS CHURCH, CITY

Corn Street **c. 1153 and later**

This church is what a small city church should really be like, full of the indefinable atmosphere of age and devotion. Surrounded on three sides by pedestrian passageways in the centre of Bristol's business area one hears little of the noise of traffic but the pattering of feet on flagstones that must scarcely have differed for the last 800 years. Not only is the entrance from one of these passageways, but the church is built into the surrounding buildings so that over the south nave aisle is a priest's room, and over the north a Georgian coffee room, still used, and part of the coffee shop adjoining. The two western bays of the nave are Norman and the next three, 15th-century, slim and comparatively lofty to form a 'hall church'. The long and narrow chancel was rebuilt in 1850. The tower was rebuilt by William Paul in 1711 and completed in 1716 by George Townesend of London in the 18th-century manner with the pretty lantern added in 1807 by Luke Henwood. The most notable monument is that to Edward Colston, founder of the Colston charitable societies and schools. Designed by Gibbs this is his only work in the city, and carved by Rysbrack (in spite of the signature of Sidnell). There is also a Flaxman tablet to Mrs Tooth Blisset, other monuments, and some fine plate.

◄ 3

▶ 4

▶ 5

4

ST PHILIP AND ST JACOB ***c.* 1193**

This is one of Bristol's most fascinating churches. It is a country church in its spacious peaceful graveyard overrun by the city sprawl. Now a traffic island, it still maintains its calm and dignity. Externally it is interesting for its swept-up gables to the west front with obelisk pinnacles and Early English tower. Internally, the arcades are unusual as each alternate pier has been removed to open up the view of the chancel, and flat segmental arches which carry on the mouldings of the pillars have been substituted. The work is attributed by Harbron to William Armstrong, colleague of Brunel, and dated early 19th century, but there is some possibility that the alteration was made during extensive repairs in 1764. The church retains its Jacobean woodwork including a 2-tier font cover, on a Norman font, and pulpit. There are some fine monuments and 17th- and 18th-century plate.

5

TEMPLE CHURCH 12th–14th Centuries

Victoria Street

This is one of Bristol's great losses through bombing, but fortunately the shell of the church and the famous leaning tower survive. The ruins are now the responsibility of the Ministry of Public Building and Works. The church was not a typical round Templar church but there are relics of an oval church of just after 1150 when the Templars established themselves in the city. The most important feature of the interior was the wrought-iron chancel screen and sword-rest by W. Edney, now preserved, but broken up into sections and re-erected in other churches. The 17th- and 18th-century plate is also preserved elsewhere in the city.

6

ST MARK, 1220
THE LORD MAYOR'S CHAPEL

College Green

This is believed to be the only church in England privately owned by a City as a chapel for the Lord Mayor and Corporation. It was

◀◀ 6
◀ 7a

built in 1220 as the chapel of the monastery of Gaunt's Hospital, long since demolished, and was purchased by the Corporation in 1541. The building is small and of great charm. The west front was altered by J. L. Pearson in 1889, but much of the original church remains in a restored state. The entrance is down a flight of steps inside the door so that one sees the church spread out below one rather as in some French village churches. There is an aisle or chapel to the south which leads to another chapel, and to the south of the chancel is the Poyntz Chapel, founded as a chantry in 1536. It is fan-vaulted in two bays and the walls have canopied niches, and there are remains of wall paintings of the early 16th century. The flat timber roof of the nave is elaborate. The glass is an odd assortment, but of considerable interest, containing some 15th-century German and 16th-century French, French Mannerist, and a grisaille by Benjamin West from Fonthill Abbey, Wiltshire. There are too many monuments to mention, some by the Paty family; a wrought-iron sword-rest and part of the gates by William Edney, salvaged from Temple Church, destroyed in the Second World War.

7
ST MARY, REDCLIFFE
13th Century and later

This church, the pride of Bristol, was called by Queen Elizabeth I 'the fairest, goodliest, and most famous parish church in England', a description with which no one has been known to disagree. It has all the appurtanences of a cathedral – transepts, quire, lady chapel, crypt, aisles to nave, quire and transepts, a vault overall with flying buttresses, and dressed stone throughout. There are remains of the 13th-century church and records exist of indulgences for its building as early as 1232. As a whole the church dates from the early and late 14th century and the earliest visible part is the base of the north-west tower of 1294. It is, therefore, roughly contemporary with the cathedral, but shows little of the imaginative break with traditional forms of construction that are evident there. The cathedral appeals to the scholarly eye, St Mary's to the emotions. The slenderness of the proportions and the tall clere-storey windows lighting the rich, cusped, lierne vault give a sense of height far greater than the dimensions justify, considerable though these are. The south aisle vault is particularly fascinating as it introduces, for the first time, ribs that are not only cupsed but curved on plan. St Mary's is then pure Perpendicular, but with an upward directional movement that is lacking in such buildings of a later date. Externally the most interesting feature is the north outer porch. The inner porch dates from 1200, but the outer one was erected just before 1325. It is hexagonal, probably to enable pilgrims to file through side doors past a statue of the Virgin but, unusual though this may be its decoration is even more so. The doorway is ogee-cusped with what can be described as a Moorish flavour, while the decoration of the wide bands around has the appearance of silver work, quite unlike that of stone decoration elsewhere of this period or before. The upper part of the spire, missing since 1446, was

▶
7b

replaced in 1872. Most of the furnishings at the east end are 19th-century, but William Edney's wrought-iron chancel screen of 1710 now stands under the tower, and there are many monuments including that to William Canynges the Younger who paid for the completion of the church including the vaulting, and the armour of Admiral Sir William Penn who died in 1670.

No comment on St Mary, Redcliffe, is complete without reference to Thomas Chatterton, that strange romantic figure who in 1752 was born in the house (part of which still stands surrounded by traffic) opposite the church which inspired his writings, and in the room over the south porch of which he used to study. It was for St Mary's that Hogarth painted his famous tryptych which now, after an adventurous career including storage for many years in a tobacco warehouse (being the only available place of suitable humidity) is now on display at the City Art Gallery. It covered the entire east end, but was removed by the mid-Victorian liturgists. The carved and gilded frame is superb.

◀ 8

8

QUAKERS FRIARS **13th Century**

Broadmead

This is all that remains of the Dominican friary that dates from 1230. There are two parallel halls adopted later by the Cutlers and the Bakers with a short arcaded link between. Also in the group is the Friends' Meeting House by George Tully, of 1747, with detailing by Thomas Paty, pretentious for a Quaker House, but perhaps emulating the nearby 'New Room' for the Wesleyans, and copying it in the provision of a central lantern. The whole group of buildings is now taken over by the city as a registrar's office and a permanent Planning Exhibition. For some reason the buildings that surround it are so planned that they turn their backs, and this pleasant oasis in the shopping area faces dustbins, packing cases and lavatory windows, while shops front the busy access roads.

◀ 9

9

ST JOHN ON THE WALL

***c.* 14th Century**

There is only one city gateway remaining, and over it stands the tower and steeple of St John's church, the narrow nave of which is alongside, built into the city wall. Beneath is a vaulted crypt, now adapted for secular parochial purposes. The crypt dates from the 14th century and the vaulting is partly a tierceron star, and partly of a richer design.

The church above is of the greatest simplicity and dignity. There is no room for aisles, but there is a shallow west gallery with painted panels. The wall shafts in the nave suggest that vaulting may have been contemplated, but this would have been difficult with no room for supporting buttresses on the outside. As it is there is an open timber roof. The furnishings are mainly Jacobean – communion table, 1635, 17th-century communion rail, font, 1624, brass lectern, about 1690, and an 18th-century wrought-iron sword rest and pulpit hour-glass. There is an excellent recumbent effigy of W. Frampton who died in 1388, and among other good monuments, a Rysbrack tablet to A. Innys of 1723.

Externally the church is obviously important in closing the vista down Broad Street with its arch and tower. It is now quite dwarfed by tall new office blocks, but that adjacent to the west side is tactfully set back so as not to conflict with the church from this viewpoint, and a junction is made at low level incorporating a

▶ 10

stepped pedestrian way. Alongside the north wall of the church is the new outlet to the St John's conduit which has conveyed water since medieval times from the top of what is now Park Street, to the old Carmelite Priory on the site of the present Colston Hall, and then on to the church.

10

ST STEPHEN **15th Century**

St Stephen's Avenue

This is, with the amalgamation of the city parishes, the Parish Church of Bristol. It is a large church of the mid-15th century, with a lofty nave and two aisles. The western tower is a tall Somerset tower with a rich Gloucester crown erected at the expense of John Shipward, four times mayor of the city, who died in 1473. The arches of the nave are high and two-centred, and there is a shallow clerestorey over. Among the monuments is one to a wool merchant, Edmund Blanket, and it would be pleasant, if rash, to believe that it was he who gave his name to the universal bed-spread. There is some good early 17th- and 18th-century silver. Meeting rooms were added at the south-east corner in 1966 by J. Ralph Edwards.

11

ASHTON COURT **15th Century and later**

Long Ashton

This great mansion, 300 ft in length, was privately occupied until just before the war, but is now owned by the city. A considerable sum has been spent on first-aid repairs necessary after years of lying empty, but the condition is still very bad indeed. Its future use is still not decided. The core is an old manor house with Elizabethan additions including a fine plaster ceiling under half the timber roof of the great hall. The big extension however was the so-called Inigo Jones wing of 1635 and this was continued in a Gothic Revival manner to complete the long south front on the other side of the gate-tower, probably once free-standing. There is also a small extension on the north-west corner of 1805 in the Gothic Rococo manner including a charming oval staircase. Internally there are some particularly fine fireplaces of various periods. The rolling well-treed park is by Humphrey Repton, who also designed much of the 19th-century building, and in the gardens are terrace walls in the form of Jacobean gables. These date from the time of the Inigo Jones wing, and are thought to have been removed from the house when this wing was classicalised.

12

THE RED LODGE **1589**

Park Row

The Red and White (now demolished) lodges stood in the grounds of the Great House built by Sir John Yonge on the site of a Carmelite priory dating from 1267. The Great House purchased by Edward Colston and used as a school from 1708 to 1861, was pulled down to make way for the Colston Hall, but the Red Lodge, much altered in successive generations still stands. The suite of three oak-panelled rooms on the first floor, completed in 1590 contains some of the finest Elizabethan panelling in England. The inner porch to the large room is extremely rich and was probably carved by an Italian journeyman. Here, and below in the reception rooms, are fine 16th-century plaster ceilings, but in the latter room, part of which was the long gallery, the effect is lost by the 18th-century extensions by John Henley though they are admirable in themselves and include a fine timber staircase.

In 1854 the building was bought by Lady Byron for Mary Carpenter, the pioneer reformer, to use as a school for girls from the streets, and when this closed was saved from destruction by members of an artists' society the Bristol Savages, who raised money to present it to the city, and themselves used it as a centre after building their 'Wigwam' or meeting room and studios out of the stables at the back. The architect was C. F. W. Dening. The building is used by the city as a very valuable extension to the Art Gallery.

◀ 11

◀ 12

13
THE HATCHET INN **Early 17th Century**
Frogmore Street

There is evidence that this building dates from the 15th century, but what has survived is 17th century with 18th-century amendments such as sash windows. Before the construction of Park Street, Frog Lane (as it was then called) was on the main route to Clifton. This was a coaching inn but nothing of the stables or yard remains. The building only escaped demolition – having survived the bombing – by being preserved in the middle of a traffic island and though still a popular pub is architecturally only a museum piece. It was altered and enlarged by Sir Percy Thomas & Son in 1967. Little of the original building remains but the façade and a decorated plaster ceiling. Once it was the resort of pugilists, and is associated with Tom Sayers, Thomas Cribb and Jem Mace.

14
YE SHAKESPEARE **1636**
Victoria Street

As with the Hatchet Inn, little remains of Ye Shakespeare but the façade. Once an important

▶ 13

▶▶ 14

▶ 15

inn and convenient for the St Paul's fair which used to be held in the streets near Temple Church, this fine half-timbered building gradually deteriorated until it became little more than a doss-house. Recently the brewery company decided to bring the building up to modern standards and, under the direction of F. L. Hannam, the façade was carefully restored and the building behind entirely remodelled.

Other half-timbered buildings in Victoria Street still standing are a group of gabled houses now used as offices and a printing works at the junction with Thomas Street.

15

ST NICHOLAS ALMSHOUSES **1652**

King Street

The street frontage is simple and crowned with a row of small gables and quite overpowered by William Halfpenny's Coopers' Hall next door.

◄ 16

Behind is a new wing built in the contemporary manner of the late 1950s by Donald Insall. In excavating for the new wing a bastion of the old outer city wall was disclosed and is left exposed to view at ground level.

16
LLANDOGER TROW **1664**
King Street
The Llandoger Trow is in a group of five half-timbered buildings (now, after the bombing, only three) at the extreme end of King Street beside the quay. As King Street was laid out in 1661 it was one of the first buildings and is virtually in its original condition, and has remained a pub throughout much of its history. Now the adjacent buildings in the block have been taken over to form a restaurant. The inside retains some fine 17th-century plaster ceilings, some original panelling, and an original staircase. The name derives from the 'Trow' or sailing barge owned by a Captain Hawkins which plied from the adjacent Welsh Back to Llandoger up the Wye Valley and the inn was the place for delivery of goods. The tradition is that Alexander Selkirk met Daniel Defoe here. Certainly is was the haunt of privateers such as Edward Teach, the 'Terror of the American Coast', and Woodes Rogers who lived nearby in Queen Square. In Victorian times it had associations with the Theatre Royal across the road, and was a resort of Henry Irving, the Terry's and Beerbohm Tree. More recently, when the B.B.C. Symphony Orchestra was based in Bristol during the war, concerts were relayed from the Co-Op hall nearby, and the Llandoger was packed every evening by members of the orchestra and many famous soloists and conductors.

17
CHRISTMAS STEPS **'Steppered' in 1669**
This is the most picturesque street in Bristol, and is one of the old direct (pedestrian) routes to the centre of the city from the heights of Kingsdown. The houses on either side vary in date, are partly gabled and partly with parapets, and are mostly dilapidated but being gradually restored. At the bottom is the remaining fragment of St Bartholomew's Hospital founded before 1275, once the home of Bristol Grammar School and later of the Queen Elizabeth's Hospital School, and at the top the tiny Chapel of the Three Kings of Cologne, founded in 1484. The new figures of the three kings in the niches are by Ernest Pascoe, and the new glass is by Patrick Pollen.

18
COLSTON'S ALMSHOUSES **1691**
St Michael's Hill
Edward Colston, Bristol's greatest benefactor, founder of the Colston boys' and girls' schools, and after whom the Colston Charitable Soci-

▶ 17

eties – The Grateful, The Anchor and The Dolphin – were founded, also founded the group of almshouses on St Michael's Hill in 1691. They were for 24 inmates, 12 of each sex, and are still used for the same purpose. In the centre between the flanking wings is the chapel with pediment and bell-cote.

St Michael's Hill is one of the most attractive streets in Bristol – steep and curving and wide, with Georgian houses on either side approached on the west off a wide pavement raised many feet above road level. Gradually the houses are being acquired by the University and are being sympathetically renovated.

19

UNITARIAN CHAPEL **1691**

Frenchay

There is a tradition that the chapel dates from 1620, but the existing building is in an almost unchanged state from between 1691 and 1720. Basically it is true to type: square (32 ft sq) with a 'west' gallery on Tuscan columns panelled in pine, two Tuscan columns supporting a central transverse beam, pine-panelled box pews, and a central pulpit cantilevered from the 'east' wall with a graceful stair. There is a wide 'crinoline' door at the entrance, but the unique feature is the 'western' tower. The tradition is that the Presbyterians, as they then called themselves, welcomed the Anglicans to their worship, the Parish Church of Winterbourne being some miles away, and the Anglicans needed a bell. This still hangs in the tower, and bears a recasting date of 1720. The building is now in a dilapidated state, but efforts are being made to repair it and much has already been achieved. Built of the local colourful Pennant stone it has great charm, and as a dissenter chapel with a tower, in unaltered state, it is of national importance.

The tower bears a weather-vane depicting Halley's Comet which appeared at the time of building, and in the peaceful grave-yard is an immense 'body-snatchers' stone', once placed on the new graves to thwart the efforts of local surgeons and their colleagues at the Royal Infirmary.

20

MERCHANT VENTURERS' ALMSHOUSES **1696**

King Street

These almshouses were built around a quadrangle, but bombing followed by the imposition of a traffic roundabout have left them with only three sides, exposed to the bustle and noise. They are homely, rendered and 2-storeyed, and

▶ 18

◀ 19

all else that is claimed in the charming poem about the kind merchants providing a home for weary mariners which is set out in gilt lettering on a board outside. Alongside these almshouses stood the Merchants' Hall, a noble building much altered by Thomas Paty in 1783, but destroyed in the bombing. This was a great loss to Bristol as it contained fine panelling in its main rooms on the first floor and was a worthy home for the Society of Merchant Venturers, still an influential society which controls many large charitable trusts.

◀ 20

▶ 21

▶ 22

21

KINGS WESTON 1710

Architect: Sir John Vanbrugh

This mansion, now in a sorry state, was designed for Sir Edward Southwell. Though small by Vanbrugh's standards, it has all his boldness of scale with the addition of one peculiar feature (repeated on a smaller scale in the Manor House at Bishopsworth), namely, the grouping of the chimneys into a massive arcade. From the ground these look modest, but from the leads they have the grandiose appearance of a Roman ruin, an appearance that was no doubt intended. The view from the roofs or the terrace to the north and west is superb, and it is said that it was a popular excursion from 18th-century Bath to watch the summer sun setting behind the Sugar Loaf in the Welsh hills over the Severn estuary. The gardens and several charming pavilions are all in a dilapidated state – where they exist at all – and the fine terrace is a shambles. Fortunately the building itself has been made weathertight, and some redecoration has been carried out inside, but its future is in doubt.

22

BISHOP'S HOUSE 1711

With the two previous residences destroyed – the old Bishop's Palace to the sound of the cathedral having been burnt in the riots of 1831 and the subsequent palace on Redland Hill having been destroyed by enemy bombs – the Bishop now lives in the earliest of the major Clifton houses, formerly the home of the architect Sir George Oatley. It has a fine segmental-pedimented doorway dated 1711, and internally the staircase hall is spacious and dignified. There is a gazebo by Oatley in the walled garden.

 ◄ 23

23
ORCHARD STREET **1717 and later**
Bristol 1

Orchard Street is the earliest group of domestic buildings in Bristol retained, more or less, in its original condition. The first houses were set out in the orchard of Gaunt's Hospital (no longer existing) in 1717, and development continued for the next 25 years. All the houses are of three storeys with dormers (perhaps not original) in the attics. Their fronts rise straight from the pavement to the parapet, behind only the shallowest of forecourts to light the basements. These retain their original iron railings which give almost the only relief to the plain façades. Partition walls are marked by strips of channelled stones and the windows generally have keystones. Some have their sash boxings exposed and some behind reveals, thus showing that the early 18th century Building Acts had reached Bristol. The door cases differ, and one or two are elaborate.

The street deteriorated into a slum by the beginning of this century but was rescued by an architect, G. C. Lawrence, and a solicitor, Meade-King, who, to the dismay of their colleagues bought houses to use as offices, thus turning the street into the most desirable professional quarter in the city. Staircases are good, and the Rococo plasterwork in 15 prob-
ably by Joseph Thomas of 1740 is typical of ◄◄ 24
the best Bristol work. The interior of 28 is altogether exceptionally fine.

24
GOLDNEY HOUSE **1720–3**
Clifton

The original house was much altered in 1860–5 by Waterhouse, though some of the interior panelling and fittings survive. The building now boasts an asymmetrical tower and steep-hipped roof. However, in the gardens the early Georgian rose-red orangery survives, though refaced in 1933, and also the Gothic circular gazebo of 1757 on the terrace still commanding views over the city to the Somerset hills. The gardens have all the features of those of a great house, but on a scale prescribed by the built-up area. There is a statue of Hercules of 1758 in the Baroque manner, a Gothic tower (to supply water for the grotto), and best of all, the grotto itself, dated in shells at 1739 (very early, surely), with waterfalls and plaster figures. The shells, in fantastic patterns and some of enormous size, were brought back by the captains of the Goldney ships. The building is now owned by the University, and new hostels are being built in the grounds, but not, it is hoped, to obstruct the views over the gardens.

25
CHESTERFIELD NURSING HOME
Clifton **Early 18th Century**
Among the free-standing houses on Clifton Hill, within yards of Goldney and Clifton Hill houses and the Bishop's House, is the wide-fronted building now used as offices for the Chesterfield Nursing Home, built in the garden behind in the most practical and austere manner just before the war by a committee of doctors. The old house is one of the finest Clifton houses though the date and the architect are unknown. It has five bays to the central portion with Ionic pilasters supporting a pediment over the central three bays, a rusticated ground-floor, and lower supporting wings on either side. Like most other Clifton houses, it is all in dressed stone.

26
DOWRY SQUARE **1727**
Hotwells
Dowry Square is open on the south side to the main road, and the other three sides are much as originally built. Chapel Row is an extension to the west side and was built at the same time, and Dowry Parade was built later to extend the east. The houses are 3-storeyed with attics, simply detailed, and with channelled pilasters to the party walls. Some of the door-cases are fine, and there is good 18th-century panelling and staircase-detailing in some of the houses. Except for one or two houses the area deteriorated badly before the war and there was talk of demolition, but by the efforts of a small group of owner-occupiers many of the houses have been well restored and it is hoped that the whole area will be preserved.

27
REDLAND COURT **1732**
Architect: John Strachan
Redland Court, now a girls' high school, was built for the Cossins family on a steeply sloping site facing south. The house consists of a central block with pedimented central feature and two linked side wings both since reconstructed. The centre block is 2-storeyed over a basement with four three-quarter engaged Ionic columns and square angle-pilasters supporting the pediment which bears a high-relief carving of four putti supporting a shield. The entrance is at the back, and the plan fully Palladian, so that in the front, facing downhill to the south, there is a terrace and flight of

▶ 25

▶ 26

◀ 27

◀◀ 28

◀ 29

steps down to the meadow. Although there is now a main road across the front and the estate was developed in Victorian times, part of the axial avenue and much of the grassland have been retained. Internally there are two good staircases, some fine panelling and door-cases, and excellent plasterwork.

28

THE MANOR HOUSE 1737

Frenchay

Architect: John Wood the Elder

The Manor House is the most pretentious of the great houses facing the Common, though the Manor itself nowadays overlooks new housing. The great houses, from west to east, are as follows – Frenchay Park (now in the Hospital, and back from the Common), the Unitarian Chapel, The Old House, Clarendon House, The New House, Frenchay House, Cedar Hall and the Friends' Meeting House; here the Common ends; then there is Frenchay Lodge, the site of Malmains (demolished), Manor Cottage, and the Manor House. The houses opposite the last three are now greatly altered, but the others are still much as they have been for the past 200 years. The Manor House has a central feature with pediment and pilasters over a rusticated plinth, with side pavilions. Most of the garden has been built over, but many of the other houses still retain their quiet old-world gardens, often with unusual trees imported by Francis Fox Tuckett, the pioneer Alpinist and botanist, who was born in The Old House in 1834 and lived there until his death in 1913.

29

REDLAND CHAPEL 1740

Redland Green

Architect: William Halfpenny

Redland Chapel is one of the purest Baroque

churches in England. It is quite devoid of Rococo influences, and has the solid, chunky feeling of a chapel by Bernini or an early work of Neumann. The architect is not known for certain, but is now generally assumed to have been William Halfpenny who was certainly working on the Coopers' Hall at about the same time. It was designed as the private chapel of the Cossins family who lived in Redland Court. Work started in 1740. The stone and the more elaborate wood carving was by Thos. Paty, all to Halfpenny's designs, and the latter in Dutch oak, enriched with limewood. Fluted pilasters internally are supported on cherubs' heads between scrolls, and the altar table, believed to be the original and found in the church recently, is a marble slab supported by an eagle with wings outstretched. The busts of John and Martha Cossins were by Rysbrack.

30

THE CORN EXCHANGE **1741**
Corn Street
Architect: John Wood the Elder

This is the most distinguished building in Corn Street and blends happily with the tower of All Saints' and the 18th-century coffee house adjoining to close the vista looking up the street. After considering several architects, including William Halfpenny, John Wood the Elder of Bath was appointed and work began in 1741. Originally the building surrounded an open colonnaded cortile, but this was subsequently roofed and glazed to provide a spacious general-purpose meeting room. The façade, of three storeys of 11 bays with the centre three bays slightly projecting, has a pediment over the centre with the royal arms and three urns. The ground storey is rusticated with vertical and horizontal channelling, and the windows are separated by giant pilasters to the side bays and Corinthian columns to the centre. The entrance is through an arched opening in the rustication. The side and rear façades are treated in a modified fashion with end pavilions, but cannot easily be seen because the sides face on to narrow passages and the back serves as a lean-to for the iron roof of the flower market, which is such an attractive feature of this part of Bristol. On the Corn Street pavement are the four 'Nails', 16th- and early 17th-century bronze baluster tables, which used to stand at the other side of the road. They were used for cash payments and are said to have originated the expression 'paying on the nail'.

31

THE COOPERS' HALL **1743**
King Street
Architect: William Halfpenny

The Coopers' Hall is the one distinguished building in Bristol's 'show street', King Street, if one excludes the Old Library which must have been superb before its enrichment was

▶ 30

removed together with its pediment, parapet and cornice. It dominates the street in scale, rising from a rusticated plinth-storey to an attic crowned by a steep pediment displaying the arms of the company. The façade is five bays wide, the central three framed by Corinthian flute-less columns standing on the plinth, and expresses the lofty assembly room on the piano nobile with its tall architraved and pedimented windows. ◀◀ 31

Internally little of its grandeur remains as for years it has been used as a fruit warehouse and auction room. However, plans are now afoot to restore it inside and to use it as a foyer and recital room for the Theatre Royal next door.

32

THE FLOWER MARKET 1745

High Street

Architect: Samuel Glascodine

The market area of Bristol is undergoing changes as new wholesale markets are being built outside the city centre. However, it is hoped and thought that the flower market will remain where it has been for 200 years, behind the Corn Exchange and All Saints' Church. Much of the market consists of an open iron roof leaning onto the back of the Exchange, but the entrance from High Street, by Samuel Glascodine, probably in conjunction with John Wood the Elder, is simple and dignified with a pediment and a Venetian window.

33

CLIFTON HILL HOUSE 1747

Architect: Isaac Ware

Isaac Ware was employed by Paul Fisher, a merchant, to design this house and included it in his *Complete Body of Architecture*. Thomas Paty was employed as mason and carver, and Samuel Glascodine (see 32) as carpenter. The house is built on a steep slope facing east

◀ 32

▶ 33

so that there is a double flight of steps at the rear leading down to the gardens. There is a central block of three storeys and two side blocks of originally one storey, though these have since been raised to two. The ground floor is rusticated and there is a shield bearing the Fisher arms with swags in bold relief in the pediment. The building is all in dressed stone. Internally the detail is similar to that shown in Ware's book, but the Rococo plastering, by Joseph Thomas, is essentially of the Bristol school. The building has for some years been used as a University hall of residence for girl students.

34
WESLEY'S 'NEW ROOM' 1748
Broadmead
It was in the outskirts of Bristol, in Kingswood, that John Wesley started his mission, and it is suitable therefore that there should be preserved here a centre for Wesley pilgrimages. The 'New Room' was begun in 1748, the architect unknown but presumed by Ison to have been George Tully. It has no street frontage, being set back in a courtyard beside the stable in which he kept his famous horse, a life-sized bronze statue of which, with the preacher upon it, by the sculptor C. A. Walker, R.A., was placed there after the faithful restoration of the chapel by Sir George Oatley in 1932. Internally it is a simple rectangle with fielded panelled galleries on three sides facing a spacious 2-decker pulpit which, with its graceful sweeping balustrades, occupies the facing wall. Three stout Tuscan columns along each side support the minister's lodging over, and an interesting feature is the octagonal light-well in the ceiling which enables the minister to survey the interior – and perhaps the congregation or even a visiting preacher – from his lodging above.

The entire absence of anything 'ecclesiastical' in the form or detailing makes this building a perfect home for the form of worship that the Wesleys introduced. The pale green and white colours reproduce the original colour found by Sir George Oatley during his restoration.

35
ARNO'S COURT 1760
Brislington
Architect: James Bridges
This is a Georgian building extended in a Gothic manner by the Quaker William Reeve in about 1760. The building is 3-storeyed with

▶ 34

◀ 35a

a rusticated ground-floor and dressed free-stone above. The parapet is battlemented; the upper windows have interlaced glazing bars and the lower ones ogee heads. Originally there was some of Stocking's best plaster work inside, but little of it now remains. James Bridges was probably the architect and Thomas Paty the mason and carver.

Across the road opposite, until the 1950s, stood the famous Bath House with Stocking's plaster on the octagonal ceiling of the great bath, but disuse and dry rot caused it to collapse and the charming entrance loggia in fanciful Gothic with an undulating façade of 14 bays between slender columns was transferred, stone by stone, to Portmeirion. At either end of the colonnade were square pavilions with ogee lead-covered domes in one of which is a door and in the other a false door carved and painted on the stone even to the extent of imitation nails and keyhole. An archway is part of the same group.

36

ROYAL FORT HOUSE **1761**

Architect: James Bridges

This Georgian house was named after the fort erected by Prince Rupert when he captured the hill from the Parliamentarians in 1643. When

◀◀ 35b

◀ 36

▶ 37

▶ 38

built it stood in spacious gardens, little of which remain now as they are occupied by University buildings, and the house itself has for many years been used as faculty accommodation. Externally it is one of the finest houses of its period left in Bristol. Internally, in spite of its unsuitable use, it still retains almost undamaged the plaster work by William Stocking, including chimney pieces, door cases, and trailing vines up the staircase walls, and some remarkable wood carvings. The gardens were laid out by Humphrey Repton.

37

KINGSWESTON STABLES **1763**

Architect: Robert Mylne

One of the most romantic groups of buildings in the neighbourhood, these stables, in their pinkish dressed stone and massive cobbles grouped around a lily-pond, were in a state of disuse and near ruin until a few years ago, when they were taken over by the Bristol police. Such alterations as were necessary are unobtrusive and the group is carefully restored. It has an almost Piranesi quality, and the simple

◀◀ 39

massiveness of scale reflects Vanbrugh's house for which the stables were built.

38
THE THEATRE ROYAL **1764**
King Street
Architect: James Paty
The Theatre Royal, Bristol, is the oldest theatre in Britain, and probably in Europe, still in regular commercial use. The Drottningholm theatre near Stockholm is of the same date, but is a private theatre and used only for festivals. The law relating to 'rogues and vagabonds', and puritanical opinion of the time led to its being built behind the buildings of King Street with no proper entrance front. The present unworthy entrance dates from 1903 and is by Pope & Skinner. However, plans are now afoot for adapting the adjoining Coopers' Hall as a foyer and to rebuild the existing entrance building as offices to the designs of Peter Moro.

The theatre is a copy of Wren's Drury Lane (long since demolished), but was made 8 ft longer. The interior was altered in 1800 when the ceiling was raised to make room for a gallery, and subsequently some of the Doric decoration was overlaid with Victorian detailing, though this does not destroy the building's unity. Since then there have been few alterations except that more green and less stone colour has been used in the decoration. The Corinthian pilasters to the stage boxes are original, as is probably the star decoration on the ceiling. The stage machinery, including the famous 'thunder run', is known to all theatre historians. Since the photograph was taken, some more of the original detailing has been revealed.

39
ST NICHOLAS **1764 and later**
High Street
Architect: James Bridges
The rebuilding of Bristol Bridge in 1764 to the design of James Bridges necessitated the removal of St Nicholas Gate, and thus of the old St Nicholas church which was partly built into it. Work on the new church actually preceded that of the bridge though it was not completed, to Bridges' design but not under his supervision, until 1769. The church was gutted during the Second World War and all that now remains is the shell and Paty's tower and spire, including the famous clock face, believed to be the only one in England with a second-hand (the works were entirely replaced). This was one of Bristol's greatest war losses as Stocking's great Rococo plaster ceiling was one of the finest in

◀ 40

England. The medieval crypt, the south wall of which is the old city wall, survived with its Whitson monument, and this and the remains of the church are being preserved by replacing the glazing and the roof and converting the building into a museum of church art.

40
ARNO'S CASTLE **1766**
Brislington
Architect: James Bridges
William Reeve, who enlarged Arno's Court in the Gothic manner, also built stables, coach house, brew house and laundry opposite the Court across the Bath Road. James Bridges was probably the architect, and he used black slag, a by-product from the Reeves' smelting works at Crew's Hole, with free-stone dressings to create a sham castle. Round and oblong towers, battlements, ogee arches and mullioned windows with fanciful cusping all help to create a building to which Horace Walpole referred as a 'Devil's Cathedral'. It is well cared for, structurally, as a club house for the employees of the Bristol Bus Company, and looks like a child's castle built of liquorice allsorts, enlarged to a giant's dimensions.

41
ST MICHAEL, CITY **1775**
St Michael's Hill
Architects: The Paty Family
It is hard to believe that this church is also designed by the Paty family, architects to Christ Church City only 10 years later. Whereas Christ Church is light and delicate, St Michael's is heavy, tough and even clumsy. Its rebuilding by Paty dates from 1775 and the interior is fully classical with aisles flat-ceilinged between moulded beams and the nave barrel-vaulted on strong Tuscan columns. There is a west gallery supported, visually, on two slender cast-iron columns. Externally the architect was influenced by the medieval tower, so that the windows, with simplified Gothic detail, and the general medieval shape to the church of three parallel roofs with gables, results in an early example of Gothic Revival rather than a genuine 18th-century church. Its importance to Bristol is in its siting rather than in its intrinsic quality. Set on the slope of Kingsdown, overlooking the old city, it gives a punctuation to the Georgian buildings climbing up St Michael's Hill, though now its silhouette is lost from several aspects against the new University buildings that hug the sky-line and spread down the slopes of the hill. There is some good plate, and some interesting monuments, particularly that to Joseph Percivall who died in 1764.

42
CHRIST CHURCH, CITY **1786**
Broad Street
Architects: The Paty Family
This church is sited diagonally opposite All Saints' across the space where the High Cross used to stand. It was rebuilt in 1786–90 by the Paty family, probably by William, and is by far the best example in the city of an 18th-century church. The interior is delicate and lofty and repainted, after war damage, under T. H. B. Burrough in what appeared to have been its original colouring of white and gold. The Corinthian columns, on high plinths to take the box pews (since replaced), support saucer domes the same height in nave and aisles, but themselves are in bare stone which probably once was finished with plaster or scagliola. There are markings that suggest wreaths similar to those on the columns of the reredos, carved by one of the Patys and rescued from the cellars by C. F. W. Dening in 1928, and erected as a rood screen. The existing rather clumsy reredos by F. Bell is of 1882. The original semi-elliptical altar rail in mahogany and iron by W. Swayne of 1791 is still *in situ*,

▶ 41

◀◀ 42

but the table made to fit it by W. and Charles Court at the same time, most charming and delicate, now stands in the north aisle. The organ retains parts by Renatus Harris and has a fine 17th-century case. The pulpit is Victorian, but the carved panels of the original Paty pulpit are retained and may one day be reinstated. There is some very fine plate.

Externally the church suffers from the removal after war damage of the shops that abutted its south side, but Paty's tower and spire dominate the centre of Bristol. The entrance is by Henry Williams of 1883, and above it are the Quarter Jacks by James Paty of 1728 retained from the earlier church.

43
UNITARIAN CHAPEL **1788–91**
Lewins Mead
Architect: William Blackburn
This important building is tucked away behind Victorian industrial buildings in the centre of the city, and new developments in the area may not improve its position. It was designed by a London architect and started in 1788. The façade has a simplicity suitable for a dissenting chapel, flat but well composed. It is dominated by a large pediment over a projecting centre portion in which is a semi-circular headed window between two smaller ones of normal shape. The base up to gallery level is rusticated and there is a pleasant semi-circular porch with coupled Ionic columns.

The interior is also simple, but dignified. The galleries are carried on iron columns, and there are still the original pews and the segmental altar rail. The mahogany pulpit is elegant and graceful. The feeling of tranquillity and space in the interior is enhanced by the flat coffered ceiling, discreetly enriched by rosettes in the middle panels from which it is hoped chandeliers will once again be hung.

◀ 43

▶ 44

44
ST PAUL **1789**

Portland Square

Portland Square is the most complete Georgian square in Bristol, complete, that is, except for some holes left by bombing and not yet filled. The 'square' itself is a rectangle, 350 ft by 300 ft, with an oval garden in the middle, and the houses are simple 3-storeyed houses with attics devoid of elaboration except for a rusticated ground-floor and the provision of a third storey, and flat pilasters to the corner houses and those in the centre of the blocks. Internally, the houses are simple and substantial without being lavish. Although built for the wealthier industrial class they have long ceased to be occupied as residences and are now mainly wholesale warehouses. The church of St Paul, in the centre of the east side, was built in 1789 to the designs of Daniel Hague, a stone mason, in a light version of the Gothic style of the time – ogee arches and all. Although the Grecian design by James Allen was passed over and though Paty might well have been given the job with far more scholarly results, the present church has a charm almost like that of a 'Sunday painting'.

45
7 GREAT GEORGE STREET **1790**

Architect: Thomas Paty and Sons

The south-east side of Great George Street is largely a poor Victorian development, but there are seven fine Georgian houses (and one other, much spoilt) built to the designs of Thomas Paty and Sons to meet the requirements of individual owners. Number 25 is the administration building of the University Department of Architecture; 23 the Diocesan Church House, and 7, the best preserved, after many years of careful maintenance by the archæologist, the late Revd. Canon R. T. Cole, is now the 'Georgian House' museum, a branch of the City

▶ 45

◀ 46

Museum and Art Gallery. The house was built for the merchant J. P. Pinney who could see from his windows his ships moored in the harbour below, and contains much of his fitted mahogany furniture and some of his own pictures, as well as a collection of other furniture and fittings contemporary with the house. An interesting feature is the cold-water plunge bath in the cellars.

46
WINDSOR TERRACE 1790–1810
Clifton
This is the most pretentious of the Clifton Terraces, and is half-way down the hill to Hotwells running along the contour. The terrace is not regular as only two central houses are finished in stone. The houses are of two extremely lofty storeys (except some where there are three of ample height) between Corinthian fluted pilasters on a rusticated plinth. As the road is private it is in poor condition and has an 18th-century atmosphere, while the end house, built on a succession of rubble-faced cellars down the side of the cliff, gives the terrace a dramatic setting from the river bank below.

47
BLAISE CASTLE HOUSE 1796
Architect: William Paty
This house, built for the Quaker banker J. S. Harford, is a solid Palladian mansion which has lost much of its supporting detail – balustrading, urns, etc. – in recent years. The interior was adapted in 1832 by C. R. Cockerell. It is now the city Folk Museum. The grounds are delightful, and are now open to the public for walks while the lower, more level part is used for three cricket pitches. Humphrey Repton designed the grounds which include all that was desired in a romantic landscape of the time – a sham castle ('Blaise Castle'), of 1766, a curved, columned orangery by Nash and, also by him, a thatched dairy in the Hameau manner of Versailles. The grounds include the wooded slopes of Kingsweston Down and the deep valley of Coombe Dingle, much of which is now incorporated in new estates.

◀ 47

▶ 48

48
THE BATHURST HOTEL *c.* 1800

Bathurst Basin

In 1821 the Bathurst Hotel was referred to as The New Inn, probably because of the New Cut and the Floating Harbour, and the hotel war and completed in 1809 to provide the docks on the river basin with constant high-water. Bathurst Basin is a locked link between the New Cut and the Floating Harbour, and the hotel overlooks the southern lock. Beyond the basin can be seen the Gingell wing of the General Hospital.

49
ST VINCENT'S PRIORY *c.* 1800

Sion Hill, Clifton

▶▶ 49 A tall, narrow house built over caves which were traditionally once a Christian sanctuary, the caryatid figures supporting the first-floor window are said to be gross enlargements of carvings in St Mary, Redcliffe. There is early glass with Christian symbols in the hall, and the upper reception room has a coloured marble chimney-piece depicting David and Goliath; that in the music-room includes Euterpe in relief. There is also a frieze on the first-floor modelled in relief from Pompeian murals now in the Vatican. Both the ironwork in the fire-grate and in the second-floor balustrade include a spear and serpent motif. The house is now owned by the artist, George Melhuish.

50
THE CLIFTON CLUB 1806

The Mall, Clifton

Architect: Francis Greenway

This was originally the Clifton Hotel and Assembly Rooms, built in 1806 for those visiting the Hot Well but preferring to live on the higher ground of Clifton. The architect was Francis Greenway, who later emigrated to Australia. Thus the interior was possibly not designed by him. The whole scheme has a façade of 19 bays of three storeys on a low rusticated plinth, the centre five bays of which project and are crowned by an attic and pediment supported on engaged Ionic columns. The bow-windows are later. Only this centre part is now used as a club, the side wings are converted to shops with flats over and the plinth is masked by the shop fronts. However, it still makes an imposing focus at the end of West Mall and Caledonia Place, twin roads of stepped Georgian houses, some with balconies, which face each other on either side of well-treed gardens. The houses of Caledonia Place retain their stone mounting blocks, now surrounded by a characterless sea of tarmac.

◀◀ 50
◀ 51

51
80 STOKES CROFT **1806–12**

Architect: D. A. Alexander

This massive building, reminiscent of the architect's more famous work, Dartmoor Prison, was built as a Baptist College, and was taken over by the Christian Scientists in 1916. Work was suspended in 1809 due to Napoleon's Milan Decree cutting off the supply of timber. The upper floors are still partitioned into bedrooms and studies for the 25 students for whom it was designed. There is a large chapel on the ground floor, but the great glory of the college was the collection of rare versions of the scriptures, second only to that in the British Museum, that was housed in the library. The building has been re-roofed with asbestos-cement corrugated sheeting but, as so often, this has weathered to a sympathetic colour that does not destroy the scale of the building.

52
THE FRIENDS' MEETING HOUSE 1808

Frenchay

The site was conveyed in 1673 to six trustees who made a declaration in 1676 that they would 'for ever hereafter permit and suffer the said piece of ground to be holden and enjoyed to

◀ 52

▶▶ and by and for the People of God now in scorn
53 called Quakers . . .' The present building dates from 1808, and among the names of wealthy trustees is that of Joseph Storrs Fry, the founder of the Bristol chocolate firm. William Penn, the founder of Pennsylvania, was a regular worshipper in the earlier church and married as his second wife, Hannah Callowhill, a Quaker heiress who lived in Frenchay Lodge next door, and the local schoolmaster Anthony Purver here translated the Bible from the original and published it in 1764 as *The Quaker Bible*. The building is in excellent condition, and retains its pine pews and panelling – by tradition unpainted – and its secluded garden.

53
THE PARAGON **1809**
Clifton
One of the Clifton Terraces, and the upper one on the cliff over the river, the Paragon is unusual in that it curves outwards over the contours not inwards as do the others. It is also unusual in the design of the porches at the rear, access side, of the sharp crescent, which are circular on plan and only quarter-engaged. On the outer side overlooking the river and facing south are delicate iron balconies, and the terrace has a well planted garden.

54
ROYAL YORK CRESCENT **1810–20**
Clifton
This is the longest Clifton Crescent, and one of the longest in England. Over the years it has fallen into semi-decay, the houses being far too

large for individual ownership. For many years they have been divided haphazardly into flats, and the exteriors have been allowed to deteriorate. Recently, pride in this noble group of buildings dominating the Clifton sky-line from far over the river has returned and, one by one, the houses are being improved. With all its gay balconies intact and painted the same colour it must have been a fine sight. The terrace stands on a wide raised pedestrian deck over the stables – used as a barracks during the Napoleonic wars when building was suspended – and the access steps are handled in a delightful inconsequential manner.

▶
54

◀ 55

55
BLAISE HAMLET 1811
Architect: John Nash
This is a complete mock, picturesque village designed by Nash for the workers on the Harford estate and happily, by some miracle, preserved almost intact to the present day. It is now the property of the National Trust and the cottages are being provided, most discreetly, with baths and sanitation, under the direction of F. L. Hannam. The cottages are grouped informally around an asymmetrical 'green' complete with village pump carrying a lantern and a dedicatory inscription. The cottages are all different in design and material, the roofs being thatched, tiled or stone slated, and the romantic sky-line is achieved with over-large chimneys, round, polygonal and diagonally set.

56
THE COMMERCIAL ROOMS 1811
Corn Street
Architect: Charles Busby
There is no work in Bristol by Soane, but the Commercial Rooms designed by Charles Busby have something of Soane's character. The building is small and overpowered by the Victorian banks on either side, and looks,

◀ 56

therefore, like a charming toy. A portico of four detached Ionic columns carries a pediment above and behind which is a blank attic that acts as a foil for three standing figures by J. G. Bubb – Commerce on the left, Navigation on the right, and Bristol, looking rather like Britannia, standing on the pediment. The interior is distinctly Soanian. The decoration is flat and the shapes are simple, and over all is a square opening supporting, via pendentives, a graceful domed lantern light carried on twelve caryatides. Much of the original mahogany furniture remains.

57
LITFIELD PLACE and LITFIELD HOUSE 1820–30
The Promenade, Clifton
Architect: C. Dyer
Litfield Place is the simplest and most dignified of the group of large mansions on the Promenade. It is, in fact, two semi-detatched houses with a 3-storeyed centre block and 2-storeyed side wings, all in ashlar. Along the whole front is a delicate iron loggia. Next door is Litfield House, with a Tuscan four-columned porch and giant Ionic pilasters over. The interiors have fine plaster and mahogany finishings.

58
THE MASONIC HALL 1821
Park Street
Architect: C. R. Cockerell
The Masonic Hall, originally the Literary and Philosophical Institution, was designed by C. R. Cockerell in 1821. It has a simple neo-Classical treatment on all three exposed sides, but the main feature is a semi-circular portico on the narrow frontage with Corinthian columns and containing a frieze carved by Baily. It was badly damaged in the Second World War and rebuilt internally.

▶ 57

▶ 58

◀◀ 59

59
ST GEORGE, BRANDON HILL 1823
Architect: Sir Robert Smirke

This is the only church in Bristol by Sir Robert Smirke, though he was also the architect of the Old Council House in Corn Street. The building has mainly townscape value as its interior is dull and at the east end considerably altered. Externally it is magnificent. Built on the side of a steep hill, one approaches the entrance down steps into a cutting while, rather incongruously, the east end is dominated by a grand Doric portico at the top of a flight of 48 steps, the full width of the building. This dramatic composition is completed by a cupola on a lofty drum set just back from the portico. Internally there are galleries all round on slender fluted Doric columns but the colours are dull greys and greens and the church lacks the sense of spaciousness that its wide unbroken ceiling would provide if the decorations were in, say, white and gold. The organ is now at the east of the south gallery where it disrupts the unity, and the chancel (if it can be called this, as it has no architectural demarcation), was redesigned in an Italianate manner, suitable to the church's Anglo-Catholic tradition, by G. E. Street, assisted by Foster and Wood, in 1871. The reredos was added by Sir Arthur Blomfield in 1876. The whole of the east end of the interior is totally unsuitable to Smirke's conception.

60
LOWER ARCADE 1824
Broadmead

Architect: James Foster

Before the bombing there were two arcades, the upper arcade from near the northern entrance to St James's Square (now mostly demolished) and the lower, a continuation of this, into Broadmead. Only the latter survives, and this only by pressure of opinion by the amenity societies. Architecturally it is fine. The entrances have fluted Ionic columns, and inside the shops have bow fronts in two storeys between other Ionic columns. It has been renovated and is let to an altogether different type of shopkeeper. The only noticeable change is the substitution of ramps for steps at the entrances, an unfortunate concession to convenience.

◀ 60

▶ 61

61
THE OLD COUNCIL HOUSE 1824
Corn Street
Architect: Sir Robert Smirke
The so-called 'Old Council House' faces All Saint's Church and Christ Church on the corners of High Street and Broad Street respectively, and is the best example of neo-Classical architecture in Bristol. It was designed by Sir Robert Smirke and built in 1824–5 on the site of the old St Ewen's Church. The planning is excellent for its purpose, but expansion in city departments has led to its being discarded for its original purpose and a new

▶ 62

◀◀ 63
◀ 64

Council house built on College Green. The main façade to Corn Street sweeps from the road line thus opening out the corner, but contemporary comments suggest that this may have been due to an error in setting-out. It comprises two lofty storeys with two fluted Ionic columns *in antis* to form a recessed doorway in the centre, and a panelling effect with pilasters elsewhere. Over the entrance the parapet is set back to provide a setting for E. H. Baily's statue of Justice, and with short Classical balustrades over the two end bays, the bays flanking the entrance are carried up solid to provide a place for panels with the arms of the city and the king respectively. The Grecian feeling is maintained inside, and provides a setting for the portraits of city worthies by Thomas Lawrence, himself a Bristolian.

62
HOLY TRINITY, HOTWELLS **1829**
Architect: C. R. Cockerell
Designed to replace an earlier church to serve the needs of the rapidly expanding Spa, Holy Trinity is an example of the architect's more imaginative approach with its giant coffered niche under a pediment as its south entrance. Originally the interior must have been splendid, with lofty Tuscan columns supporting a saucer dome, a central pulpit, putti, and decorative features partly Baroque and partly neo-Classical, but these were removed early in the century. The church was gutted in the war, only the walls and tower remaining, and as there were neither funds nor enthusiasm to restore Cockerell's design internally, an entirely new design by T. H. B. Burrough was adopted, so as not to falsify history. The memorial windows are by J. Hutton.

63
HOLY TRINITY (St Philip's) **1829**
Architects: Rickman and Hutchinson
This church stands on an important site in a fork between two main roads. Unfortunately, due to reorganisation which is likely to be permanent, traffic passes one-way beside it and no longer can its imposing façade be seen except by pedestrians. Externally its twin turrets recall Kings', Cambridge. Internally there is interesting and well-detailed woodwork, but the church has for long been unused and is in danger of demolition. This should be strongly resisted. There are some later additions by J. Bevan,Senior.

64
DORSET HOUSE ***c.* 1830**
The Promenade, Clifton
This pair of houses is notable for the high colonnaded front with oddly grouped Tuscan columns in front of a recessed 2-storey portion with a balcony on the first floor. The columns support the second floor between slightly projecting pavilions. The result is mannered and odd, but the whole effect in ashlar masonry has dignity.

65
TRAFALGAR HOUSE ***c.* 1830 and later**
The Promenade, Clifton
This is the last of the mansions down the Promenade before the later Victorian houses built of local rubble in more eclectic styles. Like Camp House higher up the road, it has a fine two-storeyed pedimented portico, with Tuscan columns over an arcade, and the side wings are Italianate rather than Palladian. The picture is completed with a magnificent 'monkey-puzzle' tree. The house is now a boys' public school.

66
CAMP HOUSE **1831**
The Promenade, Clifton
Architect: C. Dyer
This is one of the larger and more pretentious houses on the Promenade and has a wide two-storeyed portico with a pediment, Ionic above

▶ 65

▶ 66

and Tuscan below, and symmetrical side wings. The air of spaciousness is enhanced by the fine cedar trees in front and behind. Like all the houses facing the upper promenade, it is ashlar-faced throughout.

67

CUSTOM HOUSE **1832–7**

Queen Square

Architect: Sydney Smirke

Queen Square is one of the largest residential squares in Europe. It was laid out in 1699, and named after Queen Anne who visited the city in 1702. Architecturally, the square was never unified as the individual developers built to their own designs, and some of the houses are believed to have been the first in Bristol to be built of brick. However, the scale of the development was consistent because of the strict conditions of lease and, by and large, has been maintained. Less than one-third of the original buildings remain, the whole of the north side, including the Custom House, and most of the west having been burnt in the riots of 1831. Around the square are two rows of fine forest trees, but many were blown down by a freak storm on 18 November 1963 and the policy of replacement is difficult to determine. In the centre still stands the equestrian statue of William III of 1732–6 by Rysbrack, now turned awkwardly to separate two rows of traffic that pass diagonally through the square since an inner road was re-routed disastrously in the late 1930s. In the centre of the north side the Custom House was rebuilt in 1836 to a distinguished design by Sydney Smirke.

◀ 67

68
PRO-CATHEDRAL (R.C.)
Park Place, Clifton
Architects: H. E. Goodridge **1833**
C. Hansom **1847**
The original design for this church, dedicated to the Apostles, was for a noble building on an imposing cliff-edge site, with giant columns for a portico and along either side. Finance and sub-soil problems led to a halt in the building and when this resumed the columns were left without capitals and a 'chalet' roof provided with overhanging eaves supported by an ingenious system of timber posts and trusses said

◀ 68

▶ 69

to have been based on shipbuilding principles. With its Italian Romanesque Revival front the building is strange and appealing.

69
BRUNSWICK CHAPEL (Congregational)
Architect: William Armstrong **1834**
Brunswick Square is a spacious Georgian square of simple red-brick terrace houses with stone quoins and voussoirs, the west side of

▶ 70

which is being replaced by a massive development (see St James's Development, 165), while the north side has always been left open and contained three interesting buildings standing in their gardens: to the east, Surrey Villa, Bristol's most exciting Gothic toy, wantonly destroyed in the last five years: in the centre, Surrey Lodge, a tiny essay in neo-Classic with fat Doric columns *in antis:* and to the west, Brunswick Chapel, a noble chunk of masonry relieved by two pairs of tall Ionic columns. For many years it has been used as a warehouse.

70
ST JOHN THE BAPTIST **1834**
Frenchay
Architect: H. Rumley
Frenchay, a 'dissenter' village, had no Anglican church until St John the Baptist's was built in 1834. The site is ideal, overlooking the spacious Common surrounded by fine forest trees and with a background of Georgian houses. The church has a low battlemented tower with slender spire, a low-pitched nave and chancel with the same ridge, and two aisles. It is walled with the local warm pennant stone with freestone dressings. Internally the church has a loftiness enhanced by the slender moulded pillars and the plaster vault. The aisles are high enough to house lateral galleries and there is also a west gallery. The church overlooks the famous cricket ground of what is believed to be the oldest village cricket club in the world, but, since celebrating its centenary in 1946, the club has played elsewhere.

71
VIVYAN TERRACE ***c.* 1835**
Clifton
Architect: R. S. Pope
Vivyan Terrace is one of the few examples in Bristol of the 'Palace Façade' where a terrace of many houses is given the formality of an Italian palace. The central feature has eight giant Ionic columns, and the flanking features two each. The terrace is raised on a wide stone-flagged podium, and faces a private garden.

72
VICTORIA SQUARE **1835 and later**
Architects: Foster and Wood
The north-east side of Victoria Square is an Italianate terrace of *c.* 1835 called Landsdown Place. The north-west side (Royal Promenade) (illustrated) is *c.* 1840–5, probably by Foster and Sons, and the south-west side is *c.* 1855 by Foster and Wood, who were also responsible for the charming villa and archway in the south-west corner. The north-west side is in a fine, late 'Palace' style, and the south-west also contrasts strongly with the Italianate north-east. There is a delightful 'walk' diagonally through the gardens from west to east which is much used as a direct route from Clifton to the city.

◀ 71

◀ 72

▶ 73a

73

CLIFTON SUSPENSION BRIDGE

Designer: I. K. Brunel **1836 and later**

In spite of money having been given in 1752 for a bridge across the dramatic Avon Gorge, it was not until 1836 that sufficient had accumulated for work to begin; it then had to stop between 1840 and 1861 for lack of funds, and the bridge was not completed until 1864. The original design was by I. K. Brunel and work was under his supervision until his death in 1858. The work was completed by Hawkshaw and Barlow. The iron chains were from the old Hungerford Bridge at Charing Cross and it must be realised that it was built before the age of structural steel. The simple pylons in their plain rubble stone seem attractive to us today, but Brunel intended that they should be ornamented and carry sphinxes.

▶ 73b

74

ROYAL WESTERN HOTEL **1837**

(now Brunel House)

St Georges Road

Architects: R. S. Pope and I. K. Brunel

Brunel's intention was that the terminus of the London line should be at the back of the Cathedral Close in a central position, but he was overruled and the terminus had to be on the outskirts of the city at Temple Meads. However, with his ambitions of a link by steamer to America, which actually began in 1838, a major hotel was needed and the site chosen was close to that selected by him for a terminus and near the docks. 'The Hydro', as it has been called for over a hundred years, is a building in the grand manner with a four-storey façade of 13 bays, all in Bath stone, and Ionic columns to the central feature. It now looks onto the back of the new Council House over a sea of cars and ashes. If tidied up this area could be reclaimed as one of dignity and distinction worthy of a City Centre.

◄ 74

◄ 75

75
ARNO'S VALE CEMETERY **1837**
Architect: Charles Underwood
Here are two lodges and two chapels, all in the Grecian style by Charles Underwood. Greek Doric is used and the buildings have the restful eternal quality that the architect doubtless sought.

76
FARLEIGH HOSPITAL **1838**
Flax Bourton
Architects: Scott and Moffatt
These are typical almshouses of the period, designed around an octagonal core. Though unsuited for use today, and reflecting the era of cold Victorian charity, they have great charm. They are built in a soft-coloured grey rubble stone. The chapel is by John Norton.

77
ST MARY ON THE QUAY **1839**
Colston Avenue
Architect: R. S. Pope
This church really was on the quay until the end of the last century when the harbour, from the drawbridge to Demarara House (site of the new Electricity Offices), was covered and trees

▶
76

▶
77a

▶
77b

planted. This was an Irvingite church designed in 1839 by R. S. Pope in the Classical manner with a Corinthian portico and double flight of steps and must have looked fine reflected in the water through the tracery of masts and spars. Strangely, Pope was the designer also of Buckingham Chapel, Queens Road, Clifton, in 1842, in the spikiest Gothic style among sober Georgian terraces. Buckingham Place, adjoining, was also designed by him.

78
THE VICTORIA ROOMS **1839**
Queen's Road
Architect: C. Dyer
The Victoria Rooms with its giant octostyle Corinthian portico faces down Queen's Road rather as does the Madeleine down the rue Royale, Paris, but not quite, as it turns its face slightly to one side. It was designed by C. Dyer

◀ 78

◀ 79

and built in 1839–41 in the neo-Classical manner of the time; the sculpture in the pediment, representing Dawn, complete with chariot, was by Jabez Tyley. After a severe fire it was rebuilt internally to the designs of G. D. Gordon Hake and E. H. Button in the mid-1930s. While adapting it to form a first class theatre complex with level sprung floor for dances and ancillary accommodation the architects managed to maintain the Classical flavour in some scholarly detailing. It is now administered by the University Students' Union. The forecourt is by Edwin Rickards, *c.* 1911, and is a memorial to Edward VII. It is one of Britain's best examples of Edwardian Baroque with swirling steps and bronze fountains, and ingeniously overcomes the diagonally sloping site. The great gilt-crowned flag-poles in the manner of St Mark's, Venice, and so important to the composition, have been removed, and no effort seems to have been made to replace them.

79
TEMPLE MEADS STATION
Temple Gate **1839 and later**
Architects: I. K. Brunel and Sir Matthew Digby Wyatt

This is the earlier of the two stations which were combined as long ago as 1841 as the terminus of the Great Western Railway's Paddington to Bristol line via Bath. The Tudor façade facing Victoria Street still stands and the offices behind it are still used by British Rail, but both are threatened with demolition for road widening. However, Brunel's train shed behind is likely to be preserved, though for what purpose is not yet settled. For many years it was the terminus for the trains of the Midland Railway from the north via Birmingham and Gloucester, but these trains have not used it for the past five years and it is now used as an overflow car park. In view of its importance in the history of steam it is hoped that some more suitable use may be found for it. The shed boasts the widest hammer-beam roof in England, 72 ft, and this is supported on two arcades of 4-centred arches on iron pillars. The other station, at right-angles to it, is the one used today (though greatly extended), and dates from 1865–8. Sir Matthew Digby Wyatt was architectural advisor. The office building for this station built for the former Bristol and Exeter Railway also survives. It is a solid Jacobean block with shaped gables designed in 1852 by S. C. Fripp.

► 80

► 81

80
BROAD PLAIN **1840 and later**

Broad Plain is a small tree-filled oasis in an industrial area. To the south is a short row of big Georgian houses with spacious bay-windows with pilasters, pedimented doorways and one shell hood. Though they have for a long time been used as offices and stores much of the internal detailing remains including some possibly Bristol Delft tiles. To the east is a grim warm-grey rubble warehouse in the Bristol manner, now occupied by the Dunlop Rubber Company, by C. James in 1884, while to the south, beside the Georgian houses, is the large factory (illustrated), once owned by the Christopher Thomas Soap Works, designed by W. B. Gingell, and now, with the addition of a partial new curtain-wall façade by M. Hartland Thomas, is occupied as a warehouse by Gardiner Sons and Company Ltd., builders' merchants. This building retains its grandeur, though some of its Florentine skyline ornament has disappeared. It is all in brown-red brickwork and dates from the 1840s.

81
COTHAM PARK ***c.* 1840–60**

Whiteladies Road, enlarged in 1854, separates Clifton from Cotham – Conservative from Liberal – and was almost the Victorian equivalent of an 'Iron Curtain'. The Cotham houses, large, spacious and Italianate, Grecian, or with picturesque gables, are mostly in semi-detached pairs. The roads are wide and planted with forest trees as befits an area occupied by substantial merchants, but now the houses are divided into several smaller units. Cotham Park is typical of the area.

82
CHRIST CHURCH **1841 and later**

Clifton

Architect: C. Dyer

◀ 82

The main church was designed by C. Dyer in 1841 with additions in 1857 by E. Christian. In 1859 the steeple was added by J. Norton and later, in 1885, the aisles by W. C. Barret-Smith. In spite of all this the result is consistent due to the use of dressed free-stone walling throughout and the dominance of Norton's fine lofty steeple over a site of great beauty on the edge of Clifton Downs.

83
ST PETER, BISHOPSWORTH **1842**

Architect: S. C. Fripp

One of the most charming early Victorian churches, quite free of the later Ecclesiological

◀ 83

▶
84

overtones. Basically Romanesque, it has a stumpy tower with a pyramid roof and a semi-circular apse. The windows are very small and semi-circular headed and the whole appearance is as simple as possible. Inside there are two interesting pictures, the larger by D. Alexander Guvenet and the smaller by an unknown French 17th-century painter.

▶▶ 84
85 **HIGHBURY CHAPEL** **1842**
Cotham
Architect: William Butterfield
This is William Butterfield's first church, built in 1842–3 for the Congregationalists. It hints little at what was to come, but is pleasantly simple in a modified Perpendicular style with a miniature clerestorey of three quatrefoils per bay. The tower was added by Godwin in 1863. It is all of the local rubble stone with freestone dressings. Internally it is notable for the small monument to Arnold Thomas by Eric Gill, said to be the first work of his of this nature. It is carved out of the capital of one of the pillars. It was at this time, 1926, that Eric Gill was evolving his 'Gill Sans' lettering, used for the sign board of Douglas Cleverdon's book shop in Park Street, Bristol, destroyed in the Second World War.

85
THE GUILDHALL **1843**
Broad Street
Architect: R. S. Pope
THE ASSIZE COURT **1865**
Small Street
Architects: T. S. Pope and F. Bindon

These two buildings back onto each other. The former was designed by R. S. Pope and built from 1843–6, and the latter in 1865–70 to the designs of T. S. Pope and F. Bindon. Both buildings are in the Perpendicular Gothic manner, but the latter is interesting for its incorporation of a genuine early 13th-century

◄◄ 86

merchant's hall. Little if anything of this now remains, but until the wholesale interior reconstruction by the City Architect's Department in the early 1960s two arches of one of the two arcades remained with their round piers and shafting.

86

THE OLD BANK OF ENGLAND BUILDING **1844**

Broad Street

Architect: C. R. Cockerell

This is a symmetrical building with a narrow façade. Its symmetry is forced in that one of the two Grecian doors leads to the banking hall and the other to a domestic staircase to the agent's house over. It is C. R. Cockerell at his best; Grecian in its tough Doric front, but individual in that its pediment is set back over an arched attic. The ironwork with strong, thick bars has Grecian details.

87

QUEEN ELIZABETH'S HOSPITAL (School) **1844**

Berkeley Place

Architects: Foster and Son

Q.E.H., as it is known, is a boys' grammar school founded in 1586 by John Carr. The boys still wear, on occasions, their dark blue cassocks and yellow stockings of Queen Elizabeth I's day. The present building was designed by Foster and Son in 1844 and stands high up on the slope of Brandon Hill (on the grassy slopes of which the Queen restored to the women of

◄ 87

88

Bristol the right to air their washing, a right which they still exercise). It is approached by a long and wide flight of steps and is itself a handsome large building in the Tudor style.

88
ST MARY, COALPIT HEATH **1844**
Architect: W. Butterfield
This is Butterfield's first Anglican church. It shows little of what was to come, but has its own sincerity and the honest simplicity suitable for a village church. In his nonconformist church, Highbury Chapel, of the previous year, he provided small clerestorey lights, but here he squeezed the aisle roofs so closely up to the nave roof that there was no room even for these. It is built of the local rubble stone and tiled.

89
ST MARY'S VICARAGE **1845**
Coalpit Heath
Architect: W. Butterfield
Built alongside his first Anglican church, this vicarage has a picturesque charm that is ahead of its time. Gloucestershire is a long way from Kent, but it seems inconceivable that this building did not influence Webb in his design for the Red House, especially as Webb was

89

working later for Street, who carried out so ◀◀
much work in the Bristol area. This vicarage 90
was well known. It is referred to in the *Ecclesiologist* of July 1845: 'A very unaffected parsonage is building by Mr. Butterfield at Coalpit Heath, Nr. Bristol. We think he has quite succeeded in giving the peculiar character required for such a building.'

90
BUSH'S WAREHOUSE **1847**
Prince Street
This typifies Bristol warehouses, tough, strong and plain with robust Florentine detail where
it cannot be avoided. Apparently it was built in ◀◀
two stages, but the earlier part is advanced for 91
1847. Unfortunately, its future is not secure as a new road is proposed to pass over the site.

91
ST MARK, EASTON **1848**
Architect: C. Dyer
St Mark's Church, Easton, is one of the most interesting churches in Bristol. It was designed by C. Dyer but was built after his death under the supervision of S. B. Gabriel. The walls are of warm-grey rubble stone and the general feeling is Norman, but the tower is capped with a stepped pyramid reminiscent of the Mausoleum at Halicarnassos.

92
ST RAPHAEL, BEDMINSTER **1853**
Architect: W. Woodyer
The College and Church of St Raphael was the first centre of High-Churchmanship in Bristol.

◀ 92

▶▶ 94 The church, which contained an altar by Comper, was damaged in the war and subsequently demolished and the site sold. The almshouses, however, erected for aged seamen, survive, but being unoccupied their condition is rapidly worsening through inattention and the activities of vandals, though basically it is sound. They have dormers, carved bargeboards and a timber veranda along the road front. The site is delightful; the New Cut runs along the front and a small lawn at the back overlooks the harbour within sound of the shunting and the cranes.

93
THE PALACE HOTEL Mid-19th Century
Old Market

This extraordinary building, small but occupying a commanding site, is said to have been built as the Station Hotel when it was thought

▶ 93

▶▶ 95 that the terminus would be at the end of Old Market. A terminus of the Midland Line was, in fact, at St Philip's Station only a few hundred yards away, and until 1953 was occasionally used for passenger services. The hotel is unusual in retaining most of its original furnishing and fittings, including mirrors with barley-sugar pillars, though these have recently been painted over and a most un-Victorian decor generally superimposed.

94
BRISTOL GENERAL HOSPITAL
Cumberland Road **1853, 1912 and later**

Architect: W. B. Gingell

The oldest part still standing is by W. B. Gingell and dates from 1853. It is somewhat dull and in the warehouse-style of Italian Renaissance and built of warm-grey rubble stone – the ground-floor was actually designed as a warehouse. It was extended in 1912 by Oatley and Lawrence in the same materials and with semi-circular bed-balconies supported on Roman Doric columns overlooking the 'New Cut', a pleasant outlook for patients when the tide is up. Later, more functional, extensions, also by Oatley and Lawrence, date from the early 1930s.

95
LLOYDS BANK 1854
Corn Street

Architects: W. B. Gingell and T. R. Lysaght

Originally built for the West of England and South Wales District Bank, this richly ornamented building was built in 1854–8. Originally the entrance was in the centre, but later one extra bay to the left was added for a new entrance and the original one changed to a window. The detailing is exceptionally rich

even for its period, rather in the manner of Sansovino. All the sculpture was by John Thomas.

◄◄ 96

96

HOLY TRINITY CHURCH, STAPLETON

Architect: J. Norton **1857**

A typical Norton church, undistinguished inside, but commanding externally with a tall well-designed spire between symmetrical aisle gables, dominating the view up the steep Bell Hill. The church is more commanding now than it was when built because the narrow lane up Bell Hill has been widened so that approaching traffic has it in full view all the way up and it effectively closes an important vista. There is a window by Kempe, and memorial tablets transferred from an earlier church, one of which is by Flaxman of 1801.

97

ROYAL WEST OF ENGLAND ACADEMY **1857**

Queen's Road

Architects: C. Underwood and J. H. Hurst

This building, which faces the Victoria Rooms at the end of Queen's Road, together with the building erected for the Royal Empire Society, forms a minor civic or cultural centre at the approach to Clifton. As the Fine Art Academy, before the days of a municipal Art Gallery, the original building consisted of a group of six lofty galleries *en suite* in the traditional Victorian Baroque manner. The galleries were on the piano nobile and approached by twin flights of open steps in the grand manner.

Subsequently, in 1912, these were enclosed under an upper foyer by S. S. Reay, and rebuilt in marble, and an outer foyer constructed at ground-level. The upper foyer with coffered dome is decorated with large murals in the tympana by Walter Crane. Later additions, barely visible from the front, contain studios for the West of England College of Art.

◄ 97

▶ 98

98
TRINITY HOSPITAL **1857 and later**
Old Market Street
Architects: Foster and Wood
The original almshouses date from the early 15th century as recorded on the brass in the chapel to John Barstaple, who died in 1411. The present buildings, in a pleasant Tudor style around a lawn, complete with external spiral staircase, were built between 1857 and 1883.

99
QUEENS ROAD ROYAL PARADE **1859**
Architects: Foster and Wood
This was once Bristol's 'Bond Street' and is still a select and high-class shopping area, linking, as it does, the Victoria Rooms and Royal West of England Academy with the University Tower and the Art Gallery. There was an outcry when the canopies were introduced before the war as these concealed the fine arcading,

▶ 99

▶ 100

◄ 101

but, until rebuilding after war damage, the façade was kept intact in spite of major reconstruction behind. However, the City Council changed its policy and allowed buildings destroyed by bombs to be replaced to other designs both on this and on the other, later, but equally uniform, side of the street. The graceful unity of this very fine Victorian shopping street can now only be imagined.

100

CLIFTON COLLEGE 1860

Architect: C. F. Hansom

One of the new public schools founded in the middle of the 19th century. The original architect was Charles F. Hansom, who designed Big School and School House in 1860, and the Chapel in 1866. Many alterations and enlargements were made by successive generations, but all in the rose-pink local rubble. The 'Tudor' science wing, thoroughly practical and contemporary within, was designed by A. Munby in 1927 and later enlarged by Eustace Button. Perhaps the most interesting feature is the major alteration to the chapel by Sir Charles Nicholson in 1909–10, consisting of the gutting of the entire centre portion to throw out a large octagon with copper-clad timber lantern while retaining the ridge to east and west. With the Guthrie Tower, 1889, and Library as a central feature, the whole presents an imposing informal group facing the playing fields.

The church to the right of the picture is Emmanuel, Clifton, 1865–9, also in the rose-pink rubble, by John Norton, a Simeon Trust church erected to counteract Street's new church of All Saints' being erected for the Anglo-Catholic community at the same time a few hundred yards away.

101

FOSTER'S ALMSHOUSES 1861 and later

Colston Street

Architects: Foster and Wood

The Almshouses date from 1861 but the Chapel of the Three Kings of Cologne dates from 1504 and was erected by the benefactor himself. The Almshouses are in the richest Burgundian style with ornamented turrets, open spiral staircases ◄◄ 102 with candle-snuffer roofs, and projecting corner oriels. The detailing is scholarly, and the construction in diaper-patterned brickwork with stone dressings.

102

ANDERSON'S WAREHOUSE 1862

Stokes Croft

Architect: E. W. Godwin

This is one of Edward Godwin's few buildings in Bristol and his most famous. It has a solid Florentine look, built of grey rubble, with five great round arches on the ground-floor with alternate light and dark dressed stone voussoirs, and ten arched openings on each of the two floors above. A bold cornice completes the noble composition.

▶
103

▶
104

103
TYNTESFIELD **1862–4**
Flax Bourton
Architect: John Norton
Tyntesfield is the one example near Bristol of the Victorian mansion for the wealthy magnate. It had 43 bedrooms. Though some of the romantic sky-line is now simplified it retains its Gothic grandeur internally as well as viewed from the park. The chapel, most ambitious in size, was by Sir Arthur Blomfield in 1875 and is rich even for him. There is some very good stained glass in the post-Art Nouveau manner by Wooldridge. The staircase in the house was remodelled by Henry Woodyer.

104
THE COLSTON HALL **1867**
Colston Street
Architects: Foster and Wood

◀ 105

The dignified façade in the 'Bristol Byzantine' manner of 1867 conceals the fourth successive interior. From having been successively a general purpose hall for political meetings, oratorios, dog-shows and free-style wrestling, it became like a cinema in the 1930s (architect, C. F. W. Dening), escaped the bombing, was burnt down accidentally, and rebuilt under the direction of the then City Architect, J. Nelson Meredith, as a concert hall pure and simple. However, it is still used for the same variety of purposes, though as a concert hall it serves its purpose admirably. The small hall over the entrance was for many years the home of the Rapier Players, and is now, in an altered form, the home of the second company of the Bristol Old Vic.

105
CITY MUSEUM **1867**
(now University Refectory)
Queen's Road
Architects: Foster and Ponton
Affectionately known – for obvious reasons – as 'The Doge's Palace', this building was erected between 1867 and 1871 in a free Venetian Gothic style. It has great charm and quality, but the interior was entirely gutted in World War II and the present interior, by Ralph Brentnall, is purely temporary and functional and intended to last only as long as its present use is continued. It is hoped that the exterior will never be altered or demolished whatever the future of the building may be.

106
GRANARY, WELSH BACK **1869**
Architects: Ponton and Gough
The area bounded by King Street, Queen Square, and the bend in the Floating Harbour is Bristol's picturesque quarter. King Street is accepted as a museum piece, and Queen Square has its own spacious and tree-clad beauty. The space between is unashamedly commercial and the harbour is lined with tall warehouses, unimportant in themselves, but of immense value to the urban scene. Of these, by far the most interesting is the one-time granary designed by Ponton and Gough and built in 1869. This is the building that gave the name 'Bristol Byzantine' to the style, pointed arcade below, Venetian Gothic above, striped walling and Italian battlements. Unfortunately, its future is in doubt as the headroom is about 7 ft 6 in and the ventilation openings are picturesquely grilled but unglazed. At the time of writing it is partly used as a jazz club and most successfully adapted for this purpose.

◀ 106

▶
107

107
ST GABRIEL, EASTON **1870**
Architect: J. C. Neale
This church, in red brick and freestone, has a charming Frenchified feeling about the western turret and linking arcades, the pillars of which have had to be temporarily removed because of extensive settlement cracking in the walls due, probably, to the church having been built over mine workings. The church was built to serve pleasant 2-storey artisans' houses facing wide streets. They are now being swept away, and although the massive blocks of flats that replace them dwarf this little building, its dark interior with its open trussed timber roof remains an oasis of calm and religious atmosphere.
DEMOLISHED 1975

108
BRISTOL GRAMMAR SCHOOL **1879**
University Road
Architects: Foster and Wood
In the hierarchy of grammar schools this must be in the top half-dozen, especially since the time of such great headmasters as Cyril Norwood. The main buildings were designed in 1879, though the school was founded in 1532 in the old St Bartholomew's Hospital, after its dissolution. Wings were added by Sir Frank Wills and W. V. and A. R. Gough in 1909 and 1914 respectively. All the buildings are in local red rubble stone with freestone dressings, and all in the Gothic manner. A small area of playing field is retained and gives a pleasant setting to the buildings.

109
CITY ART GALLERY **1890**
Queen's Road
Architect: Sir Frank Wills
The City Art Gallery, like the University which now adjoins it, was a gift of the Wills family, and was designed by the architect member of the family, Sir Frank Wills, between 1899 and 1904. It is a typical example of Edwardian Baroque but stands well at the end of the steep Park Street vista and groups happily in this view with the later University Tower that now dominates the scene. Architecturally, there is little to note internally, but among its exhibits are the famous Schiller collection of Oriental ceramics (Schiller was one-time Town Clerk of Bristol), the immense Hogarth triptych from St Mary, Redcliffe, and much of Bristol's treasure in church plate.

▶
108

◄◄ 109 ◄ 111

◄◄ 110

110
FULLER'S COACH FACTORY 1891–1900 (now College of Commerce)
St George's Road
Architect: Edward Gabriel
This is one of the few buildings in Bristol in the Norman Shaw tradition and somehow reminds one of New Scotland Yard. It is in red Cattybrook brick and has almost a curtain wall, white-painted wooden windows occupying the whole façade between the structural mullions.

111
CABOT TOWER 1897
Brandon Hill
Architect: W. V. Gough
The Cabot Tower was erected to commemorate the discovery of the mainland of North America by John and Sebastian Cabot in 1497 (the year before Columbus). John Cabot was granted a royal pension at the hands of Richard Amerique, after whom quite possibly the continent came to be named. The tower stands on Brandon Hill, one of the several hills on which Bristol is built, and until the University Tower was built in 1925 was the most conspicuous feature on the skyline. It was built in 1897–8 in a personal Gothic style of the local red rubble stone with freestone dressings. There are four viewing balconies at the top under a short spire carrying a winged figure.

112
OLD PRUDENTIAL ASSURANCE BUILDING 1899
Clare Street
Architect: Alfred Waterhouse
This is the odd-man-out among the stone-built banks and insurance offices, since it is in hard red terracotta on a corner site by St Stephen's tower (10). It is in the rich style of the Loire Valley, though looking, if only because of its

▶ 112
▶▶ 114

colour, more like the 19th-century versions of Loire Gothic built for French industrialists and *rentiers*.

113
FLOATING HARBOUR
Since the covering of the Frome from what was once Demerara House, now superseded by Electricity House at the end of Colston Avenue, the head of the Floating Harbour has been by the C.W.S. building (F. E. L. Harries, 1905). Here the statue of Neptune by John Randall now stands. It was cast in lead in 1723 and used to stand at the end of Temple Street by the Temple Conduit for which it was made. The adjacent warehouse building with florid carving, pediment and domed turret is by S. B. Gabriel in 1894.

114
MESSRS EVERARDS' **1900**
Broad Street
Architect: Henry Williams
Possibly this is the most completely decorated Art Nouveau building in Europe. The whole façade, and the walls of the entrance recess, are tiled with off-white faience decorated with representations of Morris and Gutenburg,

▶ 113

and elongated female figures with lettering and leafy decoration. The building retains its wrought-iron gate and polished copper plates with beaten Art Nouveau lettering and swirling vegetable forms. Architecturally, it is a small building with a gable and small angle turrets with fat bulgy columns. It is thought that the architect was not responsible for the decoration, and that this might perhaps have been designed by Everard himself, and carried out by G. W. J. Neatby.

115
38 COLLEGE GREEN **1904**
(Cabot Cafe)
Architects: La Trobe and Weston
This building, The Cabot Café until the war, was the best Art Nouveau café in the city, complete with panelling, fibrous plaster, decoration and furnishing, but little of this now remains except for one or two fine fireplaces on the upper floors complete with beaten copper insets with the arms of the city and of the Merchant Venturers and one with decorative Art Nouveau formalised floral pattern inlaid in coloured woods. There is sufficient of the staircase and panelling left to visualise what the interior was once like. Externally, a modern shop front replaces the original ground floor, and the segmental pediment lost in the bombing has not been replaced. In the architect's drawing, notice the entrance doors, now altered.

◄ 115

116
ST AIDAN, NAG'S HEAD HILL **1904**
Architect: G. F. Bodley
St Aidan's is not one of Bodley's greater churches and, in fact, the nave is not completed. However, though it looks awkward externally because of the shortness of the nave in relation to its considerable height, it has a simple dignity internally that makes it worth a visit. Clustered round the east end is the vicarage, plain-tiled in the Voysey manner, and with good contemporary domestic detailing.

117
OLD 'TIMES AND MIRROR' OFFICES
St Stephen's Street **1904**
Architects: Foster and Wood
This building is hard to see as the street is so narrow, but it is one of the few surviving examples in the centre of Bristol of the Arts and Crafts movement as applied to office buildings. It was designed in 1904, and has three projecting tile-hung timber oriels carrying timber gables.

◄ 116

▶ 117
▶▶ 119

118
WESTERN (CONGREGATIONAL) COLLEGE **1905**
Cotham Road
Architect: H. Dare Bryan
This is Bristol's best Arts and Crafts building, free Jacobean with a symmetrical re-entrant L-plan facing a road corner with a gabled half-timbered wing to the side. The fine railings were a casualty of the war, but the sweeping stone boundary wall that carried them with the piers and ball finials survives. The building is approached up a hill from two sides and the lofty chimneys, spirelets and turrets create a romantic skyline.

119
ROYAL INFIRMARY **1736**
Marlborough Hill
Architects: Adams and Holden **1906**
Watkins Gray Group 1 **1969**
The extensions of 1906–11 by Percy Adams and Charles Holden represent one of the earliest examples of 'modern' architecture in the United Kingdom. With the exception of the loggias with unfluted columns on the south and west, the building is devoid of decoration and relies on the simplicity of its rectilinear massing for effect. It is built entirely of Portland stone which looks hard and white in the Bristol area where creamier stone of the Bath variety is

▶ 118

◄ 120

normal. This is one of the most important buildings in the history of modern architecture. The extensions were erected in 1969, and though entirely contemporary in manner have been sympathetically designed to fit alongside the earlier work, while the colour of the bare concrete harmonises with the stone. The lower portion to the east has a chunkiness that is admirable, but the larger extensions to the west may suffer from too many variations of concrete finish and create a restlessness that could detract from the unity of the whole.

120
MUNICIPAL LIBRARY **1906**
Deanery Road
Architect: Charles Holden
This building is of particular interest because of its date, 1906, which comes between the first and second instalments of Mackintosh's Glasgow Art School, the second instalment of which it clearly resembles. This is specially evident in the back and side elevations where tall, narrow oriels fit between flat buttresses and are supported by corbels. Internally the overmantel from the Old Library in King Street is preserved. This was carved by Grinling Gibbons and presented to the City after his death. Externally the building is perfectly complimentary to the cathedral beside it, and the same can be said of the extension of 1967 carried out by F. L. Hannam to the general design of the City Architect, Albert Clarke.

121
TOBACCO WAREHOUSES **1906–19**
The area across the river from the new Cumberland Basin bridge complex is dominated by three huge tobacco warehouses built in 1906, 1908 and 1919 respectively. They are absolutely plain, of hard red brick with blue brick plinths, and succeed in having a grandeur that might

◄ 121

▶ 122

elude buildings with a more 'architectural' treatment. The earliest building is steel-framed with unreinforced concrete jack-arching, but the second is a very early example of the use of the Coignet system.

122
ST ALBAN, WESTBURY PARK 1908

Architect: C. F. W. Dening

The earlier church, now the hall, dates from 1889 and was by Crisp and Oatley. It is in the Arts and Crafts manner and probably had some interesting detailing. The new church of 1908 is a late product of the high Victorian manner. However, it shows some personal traits which became more developed in Dening's later work. It is in grey rubble stone inside and out, and has a consistency and smoothness that is in all his better work. In section the chancel aisles with pointed transverse arches are very narrow thus creating intriguing vistas and oblique views. The reredos is by R. S. Nickson of 1937, and carved by Sir Herbert Read.

▶ 123

123
THE VANDYKE PRESS 1911

Park Row

Architect: A. Mowbray Green

This, and the building beside it formerly occupied by Savory's, the colour and fine art printers, are examples of a simplified Art Nouveau style, the former having considerable character through the warm rubble stone of which it is constructed and the detailing of the steps and railings of its street approach. Both buildings still retain some of their Art Nouveau fittings, and Messrs Savory's had a superb collection of Art Nouveau furniture, said to have been brought from Munich. The Vandyke building has recently been taken over by Bristol University and adapted, cleverly and tactfully, for the Department of Drama by Professor Douglas Jones, Burton and Farmer. The adaptations incorporate a small experimental theatre with exhibition foyer, and the new University Art Gallery.

124
BAPTIST COLLEGE 1913

Woodland Road

Architects: Oatley and Lawrence

This is one of the few important buildings in Bristol in brick – red brick with Bath stone facings. It is in the University area, beside Royal Fort and is pleasantly designed in the neo-Tudor style with tall coupled chimneys and a low battlemented tower.

125
THE WHITELADIES CINEMA 1921

Whiteladies Road

Architects: La Trobe and Weston

This was the first example in Bristol of the

◀ 124

◀ 125

'cinema group', i.e. cinema/dance hall/restaurant complex, all in one building. It admirably fulfilled a popular need of the time and all three parts of the building were busily occupied. Externally, it has changed little, but the unity of the building is lost through the various parts having been painted different colours instead of the whole building being white as it was originally.

126
WILLS MEMORIAL BUILDING **1925**
(University of Bristol)
Queen's Road
Architect: Sir George Oatley
The University Tower is still one of the dominant features of the Bristol skyline. Completed in 1925, it must be almost the last of the great scholarly Gothic masterpieces, tall and square with an octagonal lantern between pinnacles and with a crescendo of detail from simplicity at the base to the richly decorated battlements on the lantern. Inside, the grand double staircase rises under a fan vault 72 ft high to the Great Hall, destroyed during the war but faithfully rebuilt, oak-panelled and hammer-beamed (around steel trusses) to Sir George's own personal details. The adjoining wing houses the Library and was enlarged by Ralph Brentnall after the war. The tower houses 'Great George', the $9\frac{1}{2}$-ton bell which strikes the hours and is tolled on the death of a monarch or chancellor.

127
ST OSWALD, BEDMINSTER DOWN
Architect: P. Hartland Thomas **1927**
St Oswald's occupies a commanding position on one of the hills overlooking Bristol, and was built to serve a new inter-war housing estate. The architect adopted his own personal style of Gothic, with buttressed tower and pointed windows, but all in a simplified form. There is obviously the influence of the Arts and Crafts movement to be seen, but Hartland Thomas eschewed the gimmicks. The whole building is sincere, and the detailing, particularly some of the joinery, has an honest craftsmanlike quality. The walling is of warm rubble stone with freestone dressings.

▶ 126

128
CENTRAL POLICE AND FIRE STATION 1928 and later

Architects: Ivor Jones and Percy Thomas

The problems of building on this small site were great. Not only did the River Frome run across one corner, but the existing Magistrates' Courts had to be retained. Thus, the Police Station wing to the north was built first, consisting of a long two-storey building with external windows to the ground floor only, the upper floor being a very long parade gallery. Later, a 4- to 5-storey L-shaped block was built in the north-east corner for the Fire Station, incorporating 15 high doors for appliances plus a pedestrian doorway, all around an open yard for vehicle washing. The design incorporated also a tower for hose-drying.

The treatment is simple and austere in the extreme, with rather the quality of Dance or Soane. Windows are regular, recessed, and kept to the minimum. They have no cills or surrounds. Only the entrance is graced with some chunky detailing. There is not even a cornice. Altogether, it is of a far higher quality than any other major building of its time in the city if one excludes the stylistic buildings of Oatley.

129
ST MONICA'S HOME OF REST 1928

Architect: Sir George Oatley

This large institution of charity was founded by the Wills tobacco family, to rival similar institutions founded by earlier benefactors, and named after Mary Monica Wills. It was intended for elderly gentleladies in distressed circumstances and was built, regardless of expense, in a substantial 'Norman-Shaw-Tudor' manner, spreading over fields with fine trees at the end of the Downs. The chapel has the scale of a parish church and is richly detailed and furnished.

◀◀ 127

130
ST EDYTH, SEA MILLS — 1928

Architect: Sir George Oatley

This is a very individual church and displays careful thought and detailing. It consists of a nave (unfinished), chancel and two transepts, and a battlemented tower over the crossing. Externally the walling is red rubble with Bath stone dressings; internally it is ashlar faced. The chancel and crossing are plaster groin-vaulted and the nave and transepts have pointed barrel vaults. An interesting personal touch is the irregular, apparently haphazard, notching of the arch rings in the arcade.

131
PHYSICS WING (University of Bristol) — 1929

Architect: Sir George Oatley

With the University Tower this is one of the landmarks of Bristol, and is the most prominent feature on its skyline. Built in the grounds of the Georgian Royal Fort House its location possibly gave Sir George Oatley the idea of building it around a massive Gothic keep. The wings, left unfinished by Sir George, but subsequently added to by Ralph Brentnall in a much simplified style, are designed in a mansard-roofed version of the manner of Kirby Hall. The furnishings inside are as solid and substantial as the buttresses and mullions outside, and this building must be the last of a line

◀◀ 128

◀ 130

◀ 129

▶ 131

of its kind, is certainly good. The only concession to stylism, the inset columns at the top of the vertical features, reflects Charles Holden's pioneer Infirmary of 30 years earlier.

133

NEW COUNCIL HOUSE 1935 and later

College Green

Architect: E. Vincent Harris

This building has been the subject of controversy from its inception. First, because of the site. College Green is all that remains of the Cathedral Close, which until this building was erected retained some of its character though separated from the cathedral by a main road with trams, and maintained by the corporation. There was a screen of fine forest trees and the 100-year-old reproduction high cross by John Norton (the original one had been moved to Stourhead in 1764). Visually, the cathedral still dominated. Once the new building was built emphasis was turned towards it and away from the cathedral, and the felling of the trees, the removal of the Cross, the lowering of the levels and the rearrangement of the paths all focused attention on the Council House. After abortive competitions, the design was entrusted to E. Vincent Harris and work started in 1935.

▶ 132

of educational buildings built to endure. It was completed in 1929.

132

BRISTOL GAS COMPANY SHOW-ROOMS (now City Information Office)

Colston Street **1935**

Architects: Whinney, Son and Austen Hall

This is one of the few buildings built in Bristol in the pseudo-modern style of the 'thirties, and,

It consists of a wide neo-Georgian sweep with pavilions at either end and a small domed porch in the centre. There is a narrow ornamental pond in the front with simple fountains, and ornamentation is confined to two gilt unicorns (the supporters to the City's Coat) which are banished to the apices of the pavilion roofs, and a stylistic figure by Charles Wheeler of an Elizabethan sailor, presumed to be one of the Cabots, in front of the porch.

◀ 133

Internally, the ceiling of the Council Chamber is painted with a fantasy by John Armstrong, and that of the Conference Room by W. T. Monnington. The City plate and insignia, some here and some in the Mansion House in Clifton, is second only to that of London and in some respects is superior.

◀◀ 134

134
OFFICES AND SHOWROOMS **1938**
Colston Street
Architect: J. Ralph Edwards
A refined and pleasant building in the manner that succeeded the neo-Georgian (as well exemplified by the Y.M.C.A. building by G. C. Lawrence of Oatley and Lawrence, 1930, next door). It is ashlar faced throughout the street frontage.

135
ELECTRICITY HOUSE **1938**
Colston Avenue
Architect: Sir Giles Gilbert Scott
This was the last and probably the biggest office/showroom building to be built before the Second World War. It commands a dominating site at the end of the Floating Harbour, though the water has been covered in bit by bit over the last 60 or 70 years, and the building always faced traffic, paving (including the 1914–9 Cenotaph), public lavatories, and trees. It is entirely faced in Portland stone which looks hard and white beside the stone from the Bristol/Bath strata used traditionally in the city, and is the first building in the city of any size to have an underground car park.

136
THE BRABAZON ASSEMBLY HALL BUILDINGS **1946–9**
Filton
Architects: Eric Ross, Chief Architect: D. du R. Aberdeen, Architect in charge of Design
Built during the period of most acute stringency

135

immediately after the Second World War, this group of buildings is still remarkable not only in itself but in the number of ways in which it forecast trends in design later accepted as normal. The boiler house perhaps illustrates this best. The size of the project is immense – Main Hall 1,054 ft $\times$ 420 ft (side bays 270 ft); clear spans 331 ft; height 117 ft; floor area of Hall $7\frac{1}{2}$ acres; doors 1,054 $\times$ 66 ft high (electrically operated); north window-wall 1,000 ft x 50 ft high. This window has mullions designed as steel lattice beams 7 ft deep set vertically to take the wind thrust. The whole of the area is served by three 12 ton cranes with

136

◀ 137

60 ft lift supported independently of the roof structure, which itself is entirely separate for the three bays to allow the considerable movement and expansion in the steel framing.

137
REDCLIFFE HOUSING DEVELOPMENT
1950 and later

The Georgian and early Victorian housing between St Mary, Redcliffe, and the New Cut had, by the time of the outbreak of the Second World War, deteriorated into very bad slums. Bombing helped in their final destruction, and this was one of the first areas re-developed by the department of the City Architect, first J. Nelson Meredith and latterly A. H. Clarke.

The earlier buildings were in low blocks partly faced in rubble stone and grouped around grassy courts. The later buildings were more brutal; larger blocks up to 13 storeys, the one on the corner by the General Hospital being designed with an arcade treatment to the ground storey to echo the relieving arches to the road alongside the water beside which the building stands.

138
BROADMEAD SHOPPING CENTRE
(Messrs Dolcis Shop) 1952
Architect: E. Somake

Since medieval times, Bristol's shopping centre was in the Castle Street/Wine Street area north and east of the High Cross. Until the bombing, over 150 shops were here, tightly packed around the half-timbered St Peter's Hospital, the city's greatest loss in the Second World War, and the now-ruined churches of St Peter and St Mary-le-Port, all within the old city wall. After the bombing there were less than 10 small buildings fit for occupation. The city decided to remove the shopping centre to a new site below the hill where there would be more space available, and laid out the new centre along traditional lines. Buildings were designed by architects commissioned by the individual shop owners and were subject to few controls except for height. The result is visually unsatisfactory, and the one building of real merit is that for Messrs Dolcis designed by E. Somake during the worst period of licensing restrictions.

139
LOCKLEAZE SECONDARY SCHOOL
City Architect: A. H. Clarke **1954 and later**

This school is ahead of its time. Bristol and Somerset were two of the leaders in the development of 'Method Building', but this building anticipates this by several years in its modular design and treatment. The structure is a pre-cast frame with pre-stressed floors and brick panel walling.

◀ 138

▶ 139

▶▶ 140

140 **MESSRS LEWIS'S** **1954–7**

The Horsefair

Architects: Sir Percy Thomas and Son

Traditionally the Horsefair, with the Haymarket street alongside, was the Trafalgar Square of Bristol – the open space for assembly, for political speeches, processions and protests – and there was considerable opposition when it was to be built over as part of the re-planning of the Broadmead area. Nor has any alternative place been provided in lieu. On this site two of Bristol's largest shops have been built, Jones's, (Architects: Healing and Overbury), bombed out from their traditional site in Wine Street, and the newcomers, Lewis's. Both are ashlar faced, and close the north-west corner of the area. Lewis's has a rounded end with a large sun-deck on the roof with fine views over the city.

141

ROBINSON SPORTS PAVILION **1957**

Bedminster

Architects: E. S. and A. Robinson Group, Architects' Department

This is a very clean design in dark brick with an exposed reinforced concrete frame. It contains the usual changing and club rooms, the latter being fully glazed from floor to ceiling on two floors behind balconies overlooking the cricket ground. The detailing of the timber sun-shields, balcony railings, steps, etc., is most consistent and must make this one of the best post-war sports buildings.

▶ 141

◀ 142

142
ENGINEERING SCHOOL and MEDICAL SCHOOL (University of Bristol) **1958–66**
Architects: Oatley and Brentnall
These buildings, with the Physics Wing of pre-war date, occupy the skyline from Cotham to the edge of Kingsdown. When in their skeleton state of construction they gave a delicate cresting to the hill, but now, clad in pale coloured brickwork, they appear rather solid. Initiated by Sir George Oatley they were carried out after his death by his partner Ralph Brentnall. They could be described perhaps as being in a simplified neo-Georgian style.

143
ST MARY **1956**
Lockleaze
Architect: T. H. B. Burrough (of Burrough and Hannam)
St Mary's is one of the many churches built in new housing estates on the outskirts of the city. It consists of an octagon for the body of the church overlapping an elongated hexagon for the chancel and Lady Chapel. Pre-fabricated reinforced concrete units designed for industrial buildings were used throughout. Decoration is provided solely by the materials themselves (except for some stain on the woodwork), the concrete being in varying shades of grey, by the selection of aggregates, to emphasise the various functions of the parts. There is an engraved glass window by J. Hutton, a

◀ 143

◀ 144

▶ 145

▶▶ 146

particularly fine chapel window in concrete and thick glass by Margaret Trahearne, depicting the Fifteen Mysteries, a font cover by Gerald Scott, and a figure in concrete of Christ by Ernest Pascoe.

144
LOUIS WARD HOUSE **1957**
155 Redland Road
Architect: T. H. B. Burrough (of Burrough and Hannam)
This house, designed for the well-known painter and illustrator, Louis Ward, F.S.I.A., provides four bedrooms, large living-room, ground-floor study and roof studio, with a terrace and the usual offices. It is constructed of seven bays of prototype two-storey timber school prefabricated units between brick end walls. Underfloor electric heating and double-glazing units were incorporated and the structural laminated timber floor and roof beams are left exposed.

145
MANOR PARK ESTATE **1959–69**
Frenchay
Architects: Whicheloe and MacFarlane
Tucked as it is behind the Manor House this estate of 74 houses and 83 flats does not affect the character of the 18th-century village. Access is from the Old Gloster Road, close to the new motorway roundabout, thus keeping traffic away from the Common. In planning, use has been made of the fine forest trees in the park; 2-storey houses, with garages, and 3-storey blocks of flats are grouped around grassy areas with trees, rather like small commons. Garages for the flats are grouped adjacent, but inconspicuously, to each block. The walling is in brick – perhaps in rather too pink a colour for the neighbourhood. This development received a Civic Trust Award in 1965.

146
THE COUNTY CRICKET GROUND
Horfield **1960 and later**
Architect: T. H. B. Burrough (of Burrough and Hannam)
The Gloucestershire County Cricket ground, redolent with memories of W. G. Grace and selected and laid out by 'The Master' himself, still retains its original buildings in local rubble stone, so sacred that no-one would dare to alter them much, at least on the outside. However, a new reinforced concrete roof was provided over the public terrace in the form of eight hyperbolic-paraboloid 'umbrellas', each approximately 30 ft square. These are thought to be the first examples of such construction in this country and are admirably suited for their function as there are only eight supports to obstruct the view of the play, and these are well back from the front. There is also a simple extension to the old pavilion in the form

◀ 147

◀ 148

·f a row of pre-cast concrete window panels upporting a viewing terrace by the same rchitect.

47
;RISLINGTON FIRE STATION 1961
;ity Architect's Department
Not all the work of a City Architect's departnent is on a vast scale. This little fire station llustrates one of the smaller jobs to which reat care and attention has obviously been iven. The proportions, scale, and detailing are ll first-class.

48
;T PETER, LAWRENCE WESTON 1961
Architect: J. Ralph Edwards
This is the first church in Bristol designed in he new, post-war, international manner. The rchitect has been meticulous in his detailing ıot only internally but in his treatment of a curved and patterned brick wall behind the nave. To provide a sense of unity between priest and congregation the plan is almost square and undivided, but this unity is lost through the powerful clerestorey lighting on the wide altar space which throws it into prominence as dramatically as if it were a stage. There are glass and concrete window panels by Fourmaintraux. The church group is completed by meeting rooms in a wing at right-angles to the church served by a common foyer or narthex, thus forming a small paved entrance court.

149
ST CHAD, PATCHWAY 1962
Architect: F. L. Hannam (of Burrough and Hannam)
St Chad's is one of the first wedge-shaped churches, designed to provide a sense of participation for the worshippers. It contains some

▶ 149

careful detailing. The principal feature is the glass, set in resin, by Margaret Trahearne.

150
YOUTH CLUB 1962
Withywood
Architects and Building Branch, Department of Education and Science, in collaboration with the City Architect's Department.
This is the prototype youth club based on the recommendations of the Albemarle Report and was the basis for designs of subsequen clubs in Europe. The structural design of square of load-bearing brick walls and fou columns in the corners of the central well gav complete flexibility of use, and this club estab lished new area and cost standards which hav since been applied to the national capital invest ment programme. As it is situated in a built-u residential area the problem of noise, which i inherent and desirable, was acute, and specia sound-absorbent ventilating windows wer designed.

151
THE METHODIST CHURCH GROUP
Redcliffe 196
Architects: Alec French and Partners
Built to replace two neighbouring churche destroyed during the war this building expresse the best in contemporary Free-Church think ing. The various buildings comprising th group knit together but are individually dis tinctive, the church being recognisable by it treatment as well as by its size. The plan i self-evident with low-level brick walling linkin the parts and expressing the common foyer Internally the design is most imaginative, th liturgical east wall being fully glazed to presen a view of St Mary, Redcliffe, as a giant reredo over the communion table, past a great ceda cross. Within the box-like structure the churc is roofed by two hyperbolic-paraboloid shell

▶ 150

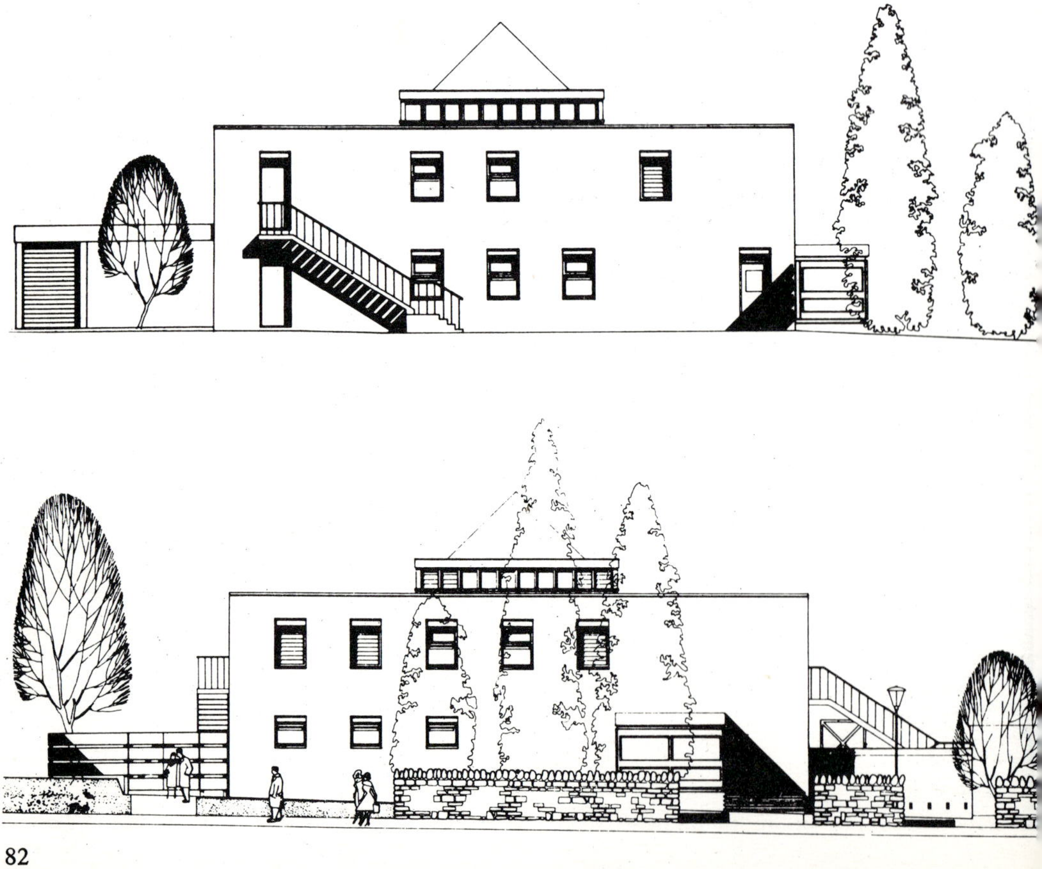

◀ 151

which also serve internally as reflectors for the indirect lighting. Only approximately one-third of the whole scheme has so far been built.

152
HOUSES AT PORTLAND STREET
Clifton 1963

Architects: Whicheloe and MacFarlane

This is a terrace of six houses, all tailor-made for individual owners, yet presenting a unified front in keeping with the neighbouring Clifton terraces. The end house links happily with the Methodist International students' house (designed by Nealon, Tanner and Partners). Inside the gates there is a delightful mews-like elongated forecourt with large ancient trees, but from the street the terrace is almost invisible behind the old stone garden wall.

153
PITCH-AND-PAY LANE DEVELOPMENT 1963–5

Architect: R. Towning Hill

Pitch-and-Pay Lane, reputed to have got its name from the days of the plague, was a pretty walk down to the river Trym from the Downs, but the area around has been steadily developed for the last hundred years as the main 'high-

◀ 152

▶ 153

class' residential district of the city and is now almost completely built-up. This small development, carried out in conjunction with Span, and in collaboration with their landscape architect, is delightfully planned so that the 44 2-storey houses are in small groups shaded by fine trees and protected by walls and planting. Construction is traditional except that the first floor is carried on stout reinforced concrete exposed beams that allow for part cantilevering.

▶ 154

154
THE ROBINSON BUILDING 1964
Redcliffe Street
Architects: E. S. and A. Robinson, Group Architects' Department

The Robinson Building was the first tower block to be built in Bristol and there is still a strong feeling that it should not have been permitted on a central site. This building opened the flood gates and there is now no stopping the rush of tall buildings that has changed the character of the city. Until 1964 the towers and spires of the city churches dominated, but these are now lost against the bulk of the office towers. In itself, the Robinson Building is a good building. It has a monumental quality enhanced by its consistency and simplicity of detail. The main block is 200 ft high of 15 floors on an open glazed foyer. Structurally it consists of a reinforced concrete service core carrying half the load and pre-cast reinforced concrete mullions faced with precast reinforced concrete cladding. Windows are fixed and the building is fully air-conditioned. The low conference wing is delightfully detailed.

155
N.F.U. BUILDING 1964
St James's Parade
Architects: Russell Diplock Associates

The Parade between Bristol's oldest church,

◀◀ 155

St James's, and the Victorian Welsh Congregational Chapel used to consist of typical Georgian terrace buildings, and the substitution of a modern office block presented a difficult problem. It has been satisfactorily solved by restricting the height to three-and-a-half storeys and by simplicity and restraint in the design. Attention is drawn to the corner details of the windows and to the projecting piinth which houses the basement windows. The spaces around the building are well handled with rubble walls, pennant stone paving and lack of sophistication.

156
CHURCH OF CHRIST THE SERVANT
Stockwood **1964 and later**
Architect: J. K. Maggs (first part in partnership with J. Ralph Edwards)
When completed (the first part has been in use for several years), this church will seat approximately 250 persons, and will have a general-purpose choir room and vestibule, and a tower, the top member of which will be finished with exposed aggregate of marble chippings from the Isle of Skye. The walls are of light grey brickwork, and the built-up copper-faced roof is supported on laminated timber beams. This

◀ 156

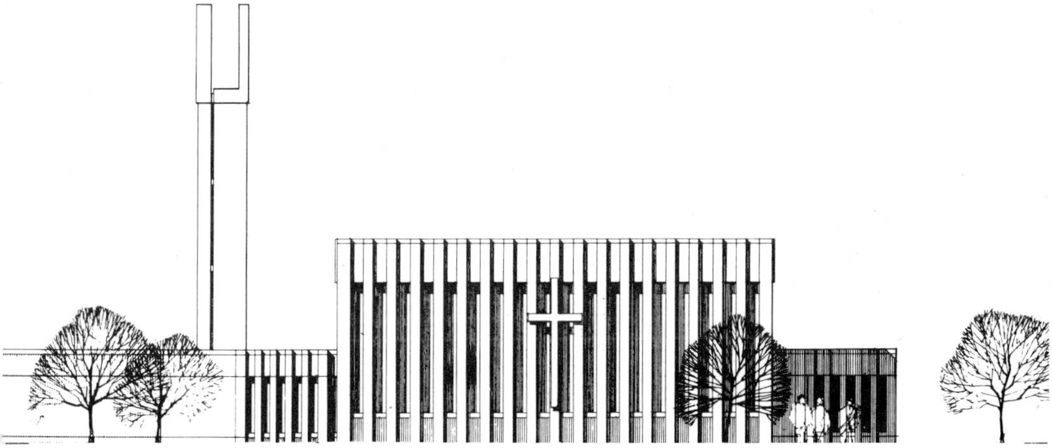

◀ 157

church should provide a focal point in a somewhat amorphous housing estate to the south-east of the city.

157
HOUSING ASSOCIATION DEVELOPMENT 1965
Stockwood
Architects: Moxley, Jenner and Partners
This estate of 197 living-units, of 37 different types varying from bed-sitters to 4-bedroom houses, is planned around a number of grassed courts of very differing sizes, though each house has its own private garden. To give life to the estate, visitors' cars are parked beside the access courts, but 100 per cent garaging is provided for residents in separate garage courts. The whole estate was completed in 12 months due to the adoption of site-factory construction. The walls are of 5 in. un-reinforced concrete slabs approximately 8 ft × 20 ft, cased externally with white sand-lime bricks, and the roof is of plywood stapled to the joists to provide, in effect, panels of tee-beams. All buildings are of one storey, and a most intimate, homely effect is achieved.

158
STUDENTS' UNION (University of Bristol) 1965
Queen's Road
Architects: Alec French and Partners
Most of the university halls of residence are two miles or so from the academic buildings, and the hilly nature of the city limits the use of bicycles. A central Union building therefore is a very necessary provision. This one is sited in an area of decaying late-Georgian property which the University is to be congratulated upon for rehabilitating for use as students' lodgings.

The building contains a 33 m indoor swimming pool, several restaurants and bars, a small theatre seating 200 (for large productions the Victoria Rooms nearby is used), as well as the usual reception and reading rooms and a hall for 700. It is interestingly planned in two linked blocks of the same height but containing a different number of floors. Externally it is clad in concrete slabs relieved by slate-slip panels, and is modelled by the provision of balconies. The handling of the ground-floor approach is excellent. Internally the standard of finish is high, and the main feature is a wide, open circular staircase.

159
THEATRE FOR CLIFTON COLLEGE
Architects: Whicheloe and MacFarlane **1965–7**
A major public school, especially one that could produce Sir Michael Redgrave, Felix Felton, and Howard Marion Crawford all from one generation, needs a theatre, but until 1967 had

▶ 158

◀ 159

to make do with the 'Big School' or other multi-purpose accommodation. The new theatre was built at low cost to seat 328 (the whole school in two houses) with well conceived stage equipment and an orchestra pit. Construction is of load-bearing brickwork and laminated timber beams.

160
HIATT BAKER HALLS OF RESIDENCE (University of Bristol) **1966**
Parry's Lane
Architects: Sir Percy Thomas and Son
Designed as two halls, these are now administered as one. Accommodation is for 440 students plus 12 tutors, domestic staff, guests, etc., and a warden's house, in social units of 12 students grouped in 3-storey blocks each for 72 students. Construction is mainly of load-bearing brick cells, the walls being of 2 in. hand-made golden-russet facing bricks, with copper-faced panels over windows and copper-faced pitched roofs. The fine trees on the site were retained and more are being planted; the buildings were sited so as not to spoil the view from Oatley's pre-war Wills' Hall, higher up the hill, designed on the traditional college staircase principle in a simplified scholarly 'Tudor' style.

◀ 160

▶
161

161
NEW CHEMISTRY SCHOOL **1966**
(University of Bristol)
Architects: Courtaulds' Technical Services Ltd.
The new Chemistry School was the first of the University's major building projects to break away from the Gothic, Tudor or neo-Georgian traditions. It is sited on the slope of the hill below the Medical School and is not conspicuous. Outside, the blank wall areas are decorated with large scale low-relief geometrical patterning in exposed-aggregate concrete, and the retaining walls to the road approach are even more heavily patterned. Internally, much use is made of coloured glazed tiling, and the building is planned around a sunken paved court with well organised changes in level. The design was illustrated at the Royal Academy.

▶
162

162
ALL SAINTS' CHURCH
Pembroke Road, Clifton
Architects: G. E. Street **1868**
Potter and Hare **1967**
This church was the first Anglo-Catholic church in Clifton, built so that the ladies and gentlemen should not have to take their carriages to St Raphael's, in what was then becoming a less salubrious area of Bedminster. It was one of Street's finest buildings, but was gutted in the Second World War, and subsequently, regrettably (as the walls were still standing), demolished. The narthex by Bodley was retained, as was the ciborium by Blacking which was never placed in the old church but was used in the church hall after the bombing.

The new church of 'contemporary' design is by Robert Potter, completed in 1967. It has rubble walls of the same red sandstone as was used for the old church, and also retains the base of Street's tower (never completed by Street, but provided with an open-work flêche

◄ 163

◄◄ 164

by F. C. Eden in 1928 which was destroyed in the bombing). The plan is intended to suit new liturgical practices and is well handled in its relation to an enclosed cloister. The window-walls are in painted perspex by John Piper.

163
CHRIST CHURCH SCHOOL 1967

Clifton

Architects: City Architects' Department (A. H. Clarke)

This is a particularly attractive example of the use of the 'method' system of building, and illustrates its versatility. It is a primary school of 280 places built in what was the private garden of a square of large upper-class Victorian houses in the centre of Clifton, hence the fine mature trees. The solid walls are faced Bath stone.

164
BRIDEWELL POLICE H.Q. ANNEXE 1967

Architects: City Architect's Department (A. H. Clarke)

The annexe far overshadows the original building by Sir Percy Thomas (128). It is an 8-storey block with basement garage, housing the Juvenile Court and Probation Officers' offices, the Crime Prevention Department, the Police School, the Traffic Police and their cars, the short-wave radio equipment and much besides. It is built on piles partly over the River Frome (they actually caught a fish in the basement), of load-bearing H-frames and pre-cast cladding. Like all new buildings in this part of Bristol, its access is from a pedestrian deck at first-floor level.

165
ST JAMES'S DEVELOPMENT 1967

Architect: R. Towning Hill

This is the largest single development in Bristol, consisting of over 200,000 square feet of office space, a bank, showrooms, a restaurant and a pub. There is a 3-storey car park over much of the site, partly underground. The building faces two streets around a corner and is over 200 yds long in total. It is of seven storeys with vertical access towers projecting above the roof line, and is constructed of reinforced concrete frame with pre-cast concrete storey-height facing panels. The building has considerable dignity though the change in colour and of surface finish in the vertical features detracts from the consistency of design. The building in no way infringes upon the Georgian Brunswick Square behind, though the last remains of the early 18th-century St James's Square left from the bombing have been demolished.

▶
165

166

BRISTOL AND WEST BUILDING 1968

Broad Quay

Architects: Alec French and Partners

Once the Robinson building had broken the Bristol skyline it was inevitable that other tower blocks would follow, and the Bristol and West Building Society building is the tallest at the time of going to press. Seventeen storeys high, there is a banking hall on the first floor off a pedestrian deck planned to link with the bridge proposed over the 'Centre'. The building is fully air-conditioned from a plant room on the roof, and, æsthetically, the building scores from its sober simplicity of detail. The cladding is of pre-cast concrete granite chip-faced panels, and the structural frame is faced with Italian marble briquettes.

167

ST BERNADETTE ROMAN CATHOLIC CHURCH, WHITCHURCH 1968

Architects: Kenneth Nealon Tanner and Partners

This is one of the more striking new churches on the outskirts of Bristol. It consists of a cluster of aluminium clad hyperbolic-paraboloids sweeping up to a central point carrying an openwork cross. The space between the lower and upper roof forms is filled with glazing to provide concealed lighting on the altar.

The plan is a square, with the altar facing across diagonally. This results in the congregation being split into two equal blocks at right-angles to one another and prevents the sense of unity and 'oneness' that is considered so desirable in church planning today. There is an organ gallery, also set diagonally, facing the altar, and well planned confessionals in the side corners. The joinery is thoughtfully designed and of high quality, mostly in imported hardwoods, but the font is the most interesting feature of the interior. It consists of a chunky

▶
166

◀ 167

square of brickwork with a cover made of ½ in. aluminium tubes arranged one on the other to form four hyperbolic-paraboloid shells supporting a cross, thus echoing the structure of the church itself.

168
BRISTOL WATERWORKS OFFICE AND BOARD ROOM BLOCK 1968
Bedminster Down
Architects: Watkins Gray Woodgate International
This is a most distinguished building standing in landscaped grounds. The fenestration is well handled to display the functions of the various parts without destroying the unity of the building as a whole. The white painting of the concrete gives the building a crispness that enhances the simplicity of detail.

169
SCHOOL OF MATHEMATICS (University of Bristol) 1969
Architects: Whicheloe and MacFarlane
Situated on a steeply sloping site in a corner of what remains of the gardens of Royal Fort House and facing the new Medical School, this building is somewhat hedged-in. It provides

◀ 168

▶
169

27,500 square feet of floor area including, in the linked blocks, a computer unit and two raked lecture theatres, and there is provision for 26 cars beneath. The building is mainly of reinforced concrete frame with buff facing bricks, and is one of the most successful of the new University buildings.

170

COLLEGE OF ART 1969

Bower Ashton

City Architect: A. H. Clarke

The new College of Art is built in a corner of Humphrey Repton's superb grounds to Ashton Court. It comprises blocks for fine arts and

▶
170

◀ 171

applied arts including pottery, woodworking and such departments, and printing, lithography, dressmaking and many other branches of art in its widest sense. There is also a lecture theatre and a general purpose theatre with stage and workshops designed in an informal way for experimental productions. There is a library and a refectory. The building is handled thoughtfully to provide interesting massing, and the immediate surrounds with steps, terraces and sympathetic landscaping are good.

171
NEW RESIDENTIAL BLOCKS AT GOLDNEY HOUSE **1969**
Architects' Co-Partnership
Goldney House (see 24) and its gardens are perched on an escarpment overlooking the city to the Somerset Hills. In planning this hall of residence it was important that the view from the terrace should not be interrupted, nor that the fine mature trees on the slope should be hidden by buildings. Blocks of 3- and 4-storeys are therefore being provided which are arranged informally in and around the trees and retaining walls, each comprising self-contained flats for six students. Internally, the finish is painted brickwork, externally, bush-hammered china clay bricks on reinforced concrete podiums. In scale and treatment the design reflects the Clifton terraces which run along the contours of the neighbouring escarpments.

172
CLIFTON (ROMAN CATHOLIC) CATHEDRAL **Due to start 1970**
Architect: Sir Percy Thomas and Son
This is probably the first cathedral in the world to be designed for the new liturgical requirements as promulgated by the Church in *The Constitution of the Sacred Liturgy* (1964). Basically it is conceived as two overlapping hexagons, so that 850 to 1,000 worshippers can be accommodated without anyone of them being more than 45 ft from the sanctuary. Construction is to be in reinforced concrete, partly *in situ* and partly pre-cast and post-tensioned. A car park for 120 cars will be provided under the floor with a lift to main floor level. Great care has been taken in the design not to dwarf the pleasant Victorian houses that surround the site, and the building should be most successful æsthethetically and in its plan form.

◀ 172

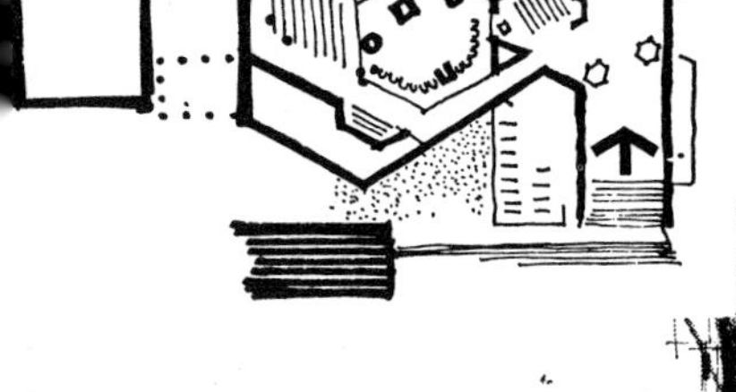

INDEX

Numbers refer to buildings, not pages

Entries in *italic* are to textual reference only to prominent architects and planners, etc., and not to any specific examples of their work.